FORM & FOLIAGE
GUIDE TO SHRUBS &
TREES

FORM & FOLIAGE
GUIDE TO SHRUBS. &
TREES

Susin Leong & Tracy Loughlin

MURDOCH
BOOKS

CONTENTS

SHRUBS & TREES

Trees tell the stories of our lives in the garden—the cycle of the seasons, the passing of the years and even of the generations. They are the souls of nature, the keepers of time. Likewise shrubs, though by definition smaller in stature, are no less significant.

When we plant a tree, or shrub, we make a commitment. It's the foundation of a garden, a vision, a place, an ideal. People have been doing it as long as we've put spade to earth—trees and shrubs have touched all corners of humanity, and they feature in our history, our cities, our cultures, religion and lore.

Trees have meaning. With shrubs, they define our gardens, homes and environments. They mark beginnings, endings and journeys. They can outlast the gardener, and certainly the gardener's whim. Here before us and here after, trees and shrubs are the milestones of our gardening lives.

Trees and shrubs are lifelong features of the garden, but they also become part of our gardening lives. Opposite: A stand of crabapples in bloom. Previous pages: A formal garden that celebrates conifers, shrubs and trees.

By horticultural definition, trees and shrubs are plants that live for many years and become woody with age. In gardens, the lines between trees, shrubs and other perennials are blurry—a shrub can grow taller than a tree, a tree can be short, and a perennial can reach great heights. Much depends on the individual plant and the garden's climate or design, as well as the gardener's point of view. In general, however, trees are known for developing a large single woody trunk (or several trunks), while shrubs have shorter trunks and usually many stems rising from the base.

Trees and shrubs are classified by their natural growing habits as evergreen, semi-evergreen or deciduous. They are also identified by their shapes. Trees, for example, may be broad-domed, columnar, conical or spreading, and shrubs may be prostrate, bun-shaped, vase-like or rounded. However, these definitions are descriptive, not strict rules, and the shapes of trees and shrubs can also be determined by the climate and the way in which the plants are grown.

A garden design based on trees and shrubs provides ornamental interest and colour, year after year. Opposite: Trees and shrubs, such as these maples and conifers, are outstanding in the garden in all seasons.

Evergreen trees and shrubs grow continuously year round, although they may slow down in certain seasons, such as winter. They don't lose all their leaves at once—if they do, they're usually under stress, such as during episodes of frost or drought.

Semi-evergreens are a transitory group, with growing habits that fall between deciduous and evergreen. Also sometimes called semi-deciduous, these plants have a partial dormancy period, when they briefly stop growing and a few leaves may fall. The behaviour of semi-evergreens can depend greatly on climate. For example, deciduous trees that originate in cool climates may not become fully dormant during warm-garden winters, while tropical-natured evergreens can lose a few leaves if grown where winters are cold.

Deciduous trees and shrubs have seasonal habits, growing and resting in a set pattern each year. Most produce new leaves, grow rapidly and flower in spring and summer. In autumn, as the weather cools, the leaves may colour, then are cast from the plant so that its branches are bared for dormancy during winter. When spring returns, the lifecycle of deciduous plants begins again.

Trees and shrubs are the structural foundations of our garden designs. Opposite: A tapestry that combines colourful foliage, flowers and form. Following pages: Trees and shrubs give a sense of permanence to gardens.

Trees and shrubs define garden designs, with their permanence, their size and also their evocative powers. Some are naturally associated with mountain ranges or woodland styles, or synonymous with coastal landscapes or tropical jungle-like settings. With their presence alone, trees and shrubs can evoke all kinds of garden scenes.

When placing trees and shrubs in gardens, many of the basic rules of gardening apply. A single tree is a feature, even numbers appear formal and provide symmetry, and odd-numbered plantings have a more natural style. Taller shrubs should be placed at the back of borders, with low-growing ones at the front and medium heights in between.

Always respect the growing habits of shrubs and trees, and keep their eventual sizes in mind. The tallest trees are unsuitable for many gardens; others may have problematic root systems or invasive tendencies. Shrubs, too, can grow formidably large, or become weeds. Although many trees and shrubs can be pruned to constrain them, constant lopping ruins their natural beauty—and removal of these plants is an unhappy event. Plan for your shrubs and trees to lead long and fulfilling lives.

When designing with trees and shrubs, always respect their natural habits and give them room to fulfil their potential. Opposite: A dawn redwood tree takes centre stage in a lawn, encircled by azaleas.

These days, many trees and shrubs are available at the local garden centre but they can also be obtained through specialist nurseries. Usually, they come as fairly mature plants in large containers or growing bags, and their cost is often determined by size, age, quality or rarity.

Commonly, they may be grafted, which means the plant is grown on the rootstock of a more vigorous species or genus. This improves its adaptability, but also encourages quicker and more reliable growth and flowering. Tubestocks, which are young plants about 15 cm (6 inches) in height or less, are increasingly popular, as they are inexpensive, establish rapidly and require less water than larger trees.

If possible, choose trees and shrubs while they are in flower or while showing leaf colour so that you know what you're getting. Remember, too, that the size of the young plant is less important than its structure. For example, a tree should have a strong, straight stem (which augurs well for a magnificent trunk), and shrubs should be well shaped, with dense habits of healthy leaves.

Trees and shrubs define the garden's style, from formal scenes and avenues to wild woodlands and groves. Opposite: This fringe tree is a feature and also sets a romantic theme in this garden design.

Before planting any tree or shrub, it's worthwhile preparing the soil. These plants are long-term investments, so give them a good start. Ideally, a few weeks before planting, the soil should be enriched with organic material (such as well-rotted animal manure, humus-rich leaf mulch, or your best compost). Turn this through the planting area, keep the soil moist and remove weeds. In containers, use quality potting mixes that are designed for your purposes. If special conditions are required, such as acidic or alkaline soil, also attend to these before planting.

Whenever possible, trial new trees and shrubs in their positions before you plant them in the garden—while still in their containers, place them in the desired spot for a few days or weeks. This helps the plant to acclimatise to your garden, and allows you to visualise the design. When planting, in the garden or in another pot, place the plant so that the soil is at the same level as it was in the original container. Grafted trees must be planted so that the graft union is well above soil level.

Trees and shrubs have an arboreal presence in gardens, and many can also be grown in containers or indoors. Opposite: Potted conifers accentuate a pathway. Following page: Flowering cherries and azaleas in harmony.

Always water new trees and shrubs gently, regularly and deeply to help them establish, especially if they are being planted during warm seasons. A very dilute seaweed-style preparation immediately after planting may also help to stimulate the growth of new roots. Mulch around the base of new plants, too, but do not let any mulch materials touch the stems.

Once settled in appropriate conditions, many trees and shrubs will simply live by the seasons, year after year, and require no maintenance. Most will appreciate regular watering during the growing seasons (for example, once a week in spring and summer, depending on the plants and conditions); however, some are naturally tolerant of drought.

Many trees and shrubs don't require extensive fertilising if they are planted in well-prepared, enriched soil, and if an organic mulch is used. A light dose of slow-release fertiliser or a top-dressing of compost can provide a seasonal boost in spring and summer. Pre-mixed formulations are also easy to use for those, like citrus and roses, with special needs.

A garden of trees and shrubs requires very little maintenance. However, it's worthwhile giving these plants a good start in the garden. Once established, trees and shrubs will reward the gardener for years.

Depending on the plants' habits and the garden style, most trees and shrubs rarely need pruning, if at all. Sometimes, however, judicious trimming can help to keep their habits tidy, or train them into desirable shapes. (For notes on pruning, see pages 485–6.) If major reconstruction is required, such as with old trees or in precarious urban situations, consider the services of arboreal experts.

Trees, especially evergreens like palms and conifers, are often best when left alone to develop their natural forms. Occasionally, lower branches are removed to provide access beneath the tree or to encourage vase-like shapes, and congested canopies may be thinned with the removal of selected branches.

Shrubs can also be left to their own devices, and many of them aren't pruned. They can benefit from the removal of finished blooms to keep them tidy, and sometimes their foliage may be cut back to encourage dense habits, or old unproductive canes removed to make way for new growth. Of course, topiaries and hedges need regular attention, but the craft of clipping is integral to their charm.

The intrinsic form of trees and shrubs can be naturally architectural in garden designs, but many are amenable to training too. Opposite: Formal box hedging and topiary enhance this liquidambar as a feature tree.

While everyone knows that without trees on earth, there'd be no life as we know it, in the garden it's a matter of choice. We plant trees and shrubs because we choose to—for shade, for harvest, for beauty. There are as many reasons for planting trees and shrubs as there are people to plant them and, without question, there is a tree or shrub for every gardening place or purpose.

This book presents a collection of favourite trees and shrubs. They are gathered by common terms—flower, foliage and fruit—but, of course, none of these plants is limited by the chapter in which it appears. And because rhododendrons, camellias, citrus and cycads are iconic, we have also honoured them separately here. The selection of plants is by no means definitive, and this title is intended only as an introduction, a guide.

Take a walk through the magical world of shrubs and trees—we hope these plants capture your imagination and inspire.

flowering shrubs

F lowering shrubs are intrinsic to a garden's character. They are naturally prolific and diverse. These plants have an array of forms, from minute groundcovers to bushes that are taller than trees, for all kinds of gardens. Flowering shrubs provide a framework for designs. As permanent features, with seasonal blooms, they will often perform without any effort from the gardener.

Flowering shrubs can create all kinds of garden designs, and they are also among the easiest of plants to grow. This page: Roses are classic, and their forms include shrubs and climbers. Previous pages: *Rhododendron* cultivar.

This chapter presents a selection of flowering shrubs that are favoured for their blooms as well as their easy-growing habits, and includes a glimpse at icons like the azalea and the rose. However, it is only a snapshot of what's available to gardeners—most shrubs will flower and so the range is endless. And, among flowering shrubs, there are blooms in all colours and seasons.

Flowering shrubs can be used on their own, but they also mix well with other plants. Left: A border featuring azaleas and viburnum. Right: Double-flowered japonica cultivar. Following pages: A design based on shrubs and perennials.

ABUTILON X HYBRIDUM
LANTERN FLOWER

From early spring throughout summer and sometimes into autumn, the lantern flower turns the garden into a wonderland with its lamp-like blooms. Large and bell-shaped, the flowers hang from fine stems and glow with colour. Fiery red, orange, yellow, pale pink, cream or white, the flower petals have a papery texture, cupped around a globe-like yellow centre. Most of the species originate from South America, but the most commonly grown in gardens are the hybrids, *Abutilon* x *hybridum*. These evergreen shrubs have open and lofty habits, eventually growing 1–2 metres (3–6 ft) in height, with large lobed leaves that provide lush foliage backgrounds for their flower displays.

The hybrid forms of the lantern flower are very adaptable in gardens. These dainty shrubs can be long-lived and will flower as young plants.

GROWING NOTES

Lantern flowers prefer warm and tropical areas; however, the hybrids will also adapt to much cooler regions. They prefer full sun, with part shade only in hot climates, and protection from strong wind. Remove flowers as they finish and occasionally trim the plants to keep them in shape. Prune plants that become rangy to promote compact growth and more flowers.

BRUNFELSIA SPECIES
BRUNFELSIA

The brunfelsia is a flowering marvel. Originating in South America and the West Indies, the genus is named, quite appropriately, after Otto Brunfels (1489–1534) who is widely acknowledged as the originator of botanical illustration, while its quaint common names of yesterday-today-and-tomorrow or morning-noon-and-night describe the plant's unique habit. The blooms of the commonly grown forms, *Brunfelsia australis* (syn. *B. bonodora*) and *B. pauciflora*, each begin life with bright purple petals that change to lilac and pale blue then almost white—a natural feat unmatched by any other flower.

GROWING NOTES

Brunfelsias are best in tropical to temperate climates; they will adapt to frost-free cool gardens but may lose their leaves in winter. They prefer well-drained soil and full sun, although they will grow in part shade. The plants need plenty of water in spring and summer. Evergreen and fairly long-lived, they will reach 2–3 metres (6–9 ft) in height and width; if required, lightly trim after flowering to maintain a compact shape.

Most of the brunfelsias create their multi-coloured flower displays in spring. The blooms of some forms are fragrant, too.

The butterfly bush is a vigorous evergreen that is very easy to grow. It has distinctive spires of flowers that attract butterflies.

BUDDLEJA DAVIDII
BUTTERFLY BUSH

Originating in China and Japan, the butterfly bush is distinguished by its towering spires of thousands of flowers which open gradually over weeks, from early summer to autumn. In the species, *Buddleja davidii*, the blooms are lilac or mauve, but, having been grown in gardens for centuries, the butterfly bush also has many cultivars. These have a range of flower colours, including white, pale pink, red and indigo, and there's also a form that has variegated leaves. Butterfly bushes can grow 2–3 metres (6–9 ft) in height, with an exuberant habit of multi-stems, and are most effective when given room to spread and display their dramatic flowers.

GROWING NOTES

The butterfly bush prefers warm to cool climates. The plants are best in full sun and rich, well-drained soil. Although they will tolerate dry periods once established, regular watering throughout spring and summer will produce better growth and flowers. Cut back immediately after flowering to encourage a compact habit, and remove old canes in winter to rejuvenate the shrubs.

CHAENOMELES SPECIES & CULTIVARS
JAPONICA

The midwinter flowers of japonica take advantage of the season's stillness to make their marvellous display. When the garden is quiet, the japonica's bare branches are suddenly adorned with blossoms of red, pink and white—sometimes a combination of all three colours. Originating from China and Japan, all species of *Chaenomeles*, and their many cultivars, are deciduous and long-lived. They grow 2–3 metres (6–9 ft) in height and have dense networks of slender upright branches that provide plenty of flowering space. Buds develop alongside spines; then, in the deep of winter, before the leaves are formed, the whole plant bursts into bloom.

The midwinter flowers of japonica may have single, semi-double or double petals, and can be red, pink or white, depending on the species or cultivar.

GROWING NOTES
Japonicas are best in climates with cool to cold winters; however, they will also adapt to warmer areas. They prefer well-drained soil and full sun, but will grow in part shade. The plants tolerate exposed, windy sites, and infrequent watering once established. Prune by cutting the flowering branches for indoor decoration. If required, remove old canes at ground level to make way for new growth.

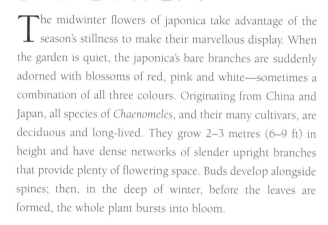

CHOISYA TERNATA
MEXICAN ORANGE
BLOSSOM

The Mexican orange blossom, as its common name suggests, originates from Mexico and is part of the same family as citrus. There's only one commonly cultivated species in the genus, *Choisya ternata*, an evergreen shrub which is grown for its profuse white blooms that are intoxicatingly scented and last for many months in spring. The Mexican orange blossom is an easy-care subject for screens or informal hedges, as well as for borders and large containers. The plants reach 2–3 metres (6–9 ft) in height, and have dense rounded habits of glossy leaves, each composed of three leaflets, and, characteristic of the citrus family, the foliage is aromatic.

GROWING NOTES

The Mexican orange blossom grows in climates from warm to cool, and also suits mild coastal conditions. Although the plants do tolerate light frost, in colder regions they are best in sheltered positions. They prefer full sun and rich, well-drained soil. Water regularly throughout warm seasons. Pruning is not essential; however, plants may be trimmed after flowering to keep them tidy, or clipped into more formal shapes.

The Mexican orange blossom suits many garden situations and styles. These trouble-free shrubs are fast-growing and will flower as young plants.

CISTUS SPECIES & HYBRIDS
ROCK ROSE

The flowers of the rock rose look fragile but these evergreen shrubs from the Mediterranean region are actually very tough. The rock rose will tolerate coastal conditions, strong winds, poor soils, frost and drought. The plants live long but flower young, and profusely. Most of the *Cistus* species, as well as their many cultivars and hybrids, have open unstructured habits and will grow about 60 cm–2 metres (2–6 ft) in height. Their leaves are generally dark green and lance-shaped, a perfect foil for the spectacular blooms of magenta, pink, lilac or white papery petals around glowing yellow centres.

GROWING NOTES

Rock roses prefer climates with hot, dry summers and cool, wet winters, similar to their Mediterranean origins. The plants need full sun and well-drained soil. They struggle in areas with high summer rainfall or humidity, or in heavy or waterlogged soils. Once established, the plants don't need regular watering. Tip-pruning of young plants helps to keep their habits dense and tidy; older shrubs can be cut back after flowering.

The rock rose has a lax and open habit that forms a drift of foliage and flowers. These shrubs suit mixed borders, informal screens and hedges.

COLEONEMA SPECIES & CULTIVARS
DIOSMA

The pink diosma blooms from midwinter through spring. Both the foliage and flowers of these shrubs are lightly fragrant.

The colourful misty appearance of diosmas in bloom is composed of thousands of tiny starry flowers which blanket the plant, almost obscuring its foliage, in winter and spring. In gardens, the cloud-like effect is enhanced when diosmas are planted in groups, as in hedges and drifts, but they also suit mixed borders and pots. Of these evergreen shrubs from South Africa, the most commonly grown species is *Coleonema pulchrum*, the pink diosma. It includes varieties with flower colours from almost red to lilac, as well as the dwarf cultivar 'Sunset Gold', which has foliage with yellow tones. Also popular is the white diosma, *C. album*, which flowers mainly in spring but also intermittently throughout the year.

GROWING NOTES

Diosmas are best in frost-free, tropical to warm climates. The plants require full sun to develop dense growth and profuse displays of flowers. The soil must be well drained, as diosmas are very susceptible to root rot. Water regularly to establish, then do not overwater. Prune the plants immediately after flowering, and lightly trim in summer to keep them shapely.

DAPHNE SPECIES & CULTIVARS
DAPHNE

Daphnes are often planted in our gardens close to our homes, where their winter and early spring flowers are always welcome and their scent can be most appreciated. Beside pathways, under windows and in pots, daphnes are very suitable shrubs for intimate garden situations. Most of them grow no more than 1 metre (3 ft) in height, with ovate glossy leaves and lush habits—but gardeners should be aware that all parts of these tempting plants are poisonous. There are many types of daphne commonly cultivated, depending on the garden's climate. The sweet daphne, *Daphne odora*, is best in warmer gardens, while the low-growing *D. cneorum* and the hybrid *D.* x *burkwoodii* prefer cooler regions.

GROWING NOTES

Daphnes suit various climates, but aren't suitable for the tropics. They require filtered sunlight or part shade with morning sun only. The soil must be very well drained and enriched with organic matter. The plants like to have cool roots, but are extremely susceptible to root rot and overwatering. The shrubs rarely need pruning; cutting flower sprigs to bring indoors is enough to keep them compact.

Most of the daphnes have clusters of star-shaped, waxy, pale pink flowers and bright red buds. However, there are also cultivars with white flowers or variegated leaves.

DEUTZIA SPECIES

WEDDING BELLS

Originating in China and Japan, *Deutzia* is a genus of deciduous shrubs that flower in spring with a flourish of tiny white bells that give the plants their common name. As well as numerous species, there are also many cultivars, some with double-petalled flowers or pale pink blooms. Long-lived but flowering from a young age, these shrubs grow 1–3 metres (3–9 ft) in height, depending on the type. They are ideal in woodland understoreys, mixed borders or shrubberies, and have dense habits of slightly furry, light green leaves which can take on dark burgundy autumn tones.

Wedding bells will flower for weeks in spring. These shrubs have many fine branches that enhance their displays of bloom.

GROWING NOTES

These shrubs are easy to grow in cool and temperate climates where they prefer full sun. They adapt to warmer regions, if slightly shaded and protected from hot sun and dry wind, but are unsuitable for tropical areas. The soil should be well drained and quite rich. Water plants regularly in warm weather. Trim flowerheads after they finish; if required, remove older canes at ground level to promote new growth.

ECHIUM CANDICANS
PRIDE OF MADEIRA

Hundreds of flowers conspire to create the giant panicle which transforms the pride of Madeira into a garden spectacular. An evergreen shrub with a sprawling constitution, *Echium candicans* (syn. *E. fastuosum*) grows to about 1.5 metres (5 ft) in height and spreads much wider, but is long-lived only in Mediterranean-type climates. The plant is multi-stemmed, with whorls of large grey-green leaves that provide a dramatic background for the brilliant blue flowers. With each shrub capable of producing many panicles, the pride of Madeira should never be confined to poky garden places. It thrives in open aspects and coastal conditions, and should be planted where it can tower towards the sun.

GROWING NOTES

The pride of Madeira prefers warm climates with dry summers but also grows in cooler regions if protected from heavy frost. These plants require full sun all day, excellent air circulation, and very well drained soil. They are particularly successful in soils that are poor quality, rocky or sandy. To keep plants compact, remove finished flower stems and, if required, trim the foliage during the growing season.

Echium candicans will flower from spring to early summer; it is also commonly known as the tower of jewels.

HEATHS & HEATHER

There are hundreds of heaths in cultivation, all with bell-shaped flowers. These cover the shrubs, creating their typically misty appearance.

The heaths are a remarkably prolific genus of shrubs, with more than 750 known species distributed throughout Europe and South Africa. Although most species (about 500) come from the Cape region of South Africa, heaths are also synonymous with the heathlands of Europe and are definitive of these landscapes by natural abundance and by name.

All species of *Erica* are typified by their flowers, which are bell-shaped or tubular, with the petals fused into a five-lobed corolla. These plants, however, are diverse in habit: while most heaths are generally shrubby, some species can grow into trees that are 5 metres (15 ft) tall, or they may form low mounds less than 60 cm (2 ft) in height. For centuries, gardeners have fiddled with the wild heaths and many cultivars now exist. Apart from their amazing range of flower colours—including white, pink, purple, orange and red, as well as two-tones—heaths will bloom in various seasons, so they can be selected to create year-round displays.

Closely related to the heaths is the heather, *Calluna vulgaris*, and although there is only one species in the genus, it is

incredibly variable. Many forms of heather are found in the wild and also in cultivation, including the white heather, which has been associated with Scottish culture and with good luck for hundreds of years.

GROWING NOTES

The heaths (and heathers) are best in cool, dry climates, but some will adapt to warmer regions. All heaths must have acidic soil; however, *E. carnea* will tolerate slightly limey conditions. They require full sun and good air circulation. The soil must be very well drained and enriched with organic matter. Heaths quickly succumb to root rot, overwatering or high humidity. Plants can be tip-pruned after flowering, but avoid cutting the older wood which won't re-grow.

Although they suit mixed borders and rockeries, heaths can be effectively planted on their own. With a range of flower colours in all seasons, they form a spectacular tapestry.

FUCHSIA SPECIES & CULTIVARS
FUCHSIA

From a few species, such as *Fuchsia magellanica* (above) and *F. triphylla* (right), there are thousands of hybrids and cultivars. Most fuchsias will flower from summer to autumn.

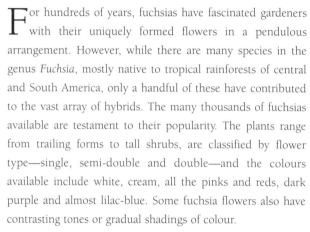

For hundreds of years, fuchsias have fascinated gardeners with their uniquely formed flowers in a pendulous arrangement. However, while there are many species in the genus *Fuchsia*, mostly native to tropical rainforests of central and South America, only a handful of these have contributed to the vast array of hybrids. The many thousands of fuchsias available are testament to their popularity. The plants range from trailing forms to tall shrubs, are classified by flower type—single, semi-double and double—and the colours available include white, cream, all the pinks and reds, dark purple and almost lilac-blue. Some fuchsia flowers also have contrasting tones or gradual shadings of colour.

GROWING NOTES

Most fuchsias adapt to a wide range of conditions from cool to subtropical. Some types are herbaceous and frost hardy, while others are tender and need to spend cold winters indoors. All fuchsias prefer dappled or part shade and sheltered conditions. Tip-pruning will encourage compact growth and more flowers. Older, straggly plants may be cut back at the end of winter.

GARDENIA AUGUSTA
GARDENIA

Gardenias are famous for their fragrant white flowers throughout late spring and summer, but these plants also have many uses in garden designs, from informal hedges to pots.

Glossy-leaved, with luscious flowers glistening white and that incomparable perfume, the gardenias have many attractions, and the plants are also easy to grow. Originating in China, *Gardenia augusta* is immensely popular in warm climates all over the world. These evergreen shrubs will thrive in frost-free gardens as well as pots, but may also be grown indoors. The plants are long-lived, maturing at about 2 metres (6 ft) in height after a few years, but flower when very young. There are several cultivars, including some, like 'Grandiflora' and 'Magnifica', with larger-than-normal blooms; as well as 'Radicans', which grows less than 30 cm (1 ft) in height, with a spreading habit that effectively displays its flowers.

GROWING NOTES

Gardenias prefer warm to tropical climates, but can also be grown in cool regions in conservatories. They are best in morning sun or dappled shade; the plants are prone to sunburn, while heavy shade results in sparse growth and few flowers. The soil must be well drained and preferably slightly acidic. Tip-prune immediately after flowering to tidy the plants or keep them in shape.

HEBE SPECIES & CULTIVARS
HEBE

The hebes were one of the first plants from New Zealand to hit mainstream horticulture, after the English plant collector, Allan Cunningham, sent the first seeds of *Hebe* to Britain in the late 1800s. The hebe, sometimes known as speedwell, quickly became popular, and today there are many species, cultivars and hybrids for gardens. Evergreen, hebes generally grow 1–2 metres (3–6 ft) in height, and are often used in mixed borders or as low, informal hedges. Some of the smaller types can also be grown in pots. One of their best assets is their suitability for coastal gardens, and many hebes are extremely tolerant of sandy soil, salt and sea spray.

GROWING NOTES

Most hebes are best in warm to cool climates; however, some will tolerate light frost or will grow in tropical conditions. The plants must have full sun, open aspects and well-drained soil. They are prone to root rot in heavy soils. Water regularly to establish, after which the plants will withstand dry periods. Prune after flowering to keep them growing densely.

Most hebes have a long flowering season, usually from spring throughout summer and into early autumn; the brushes of flowers may be white, pink, red, purple or blue.

HELIOTROPIUM ARBORESCENS
HELIOTROPE

Heliotropes flower from spring throughout summer. The shrubs are cloaked in clusters of bloom and a sweet vanilla aroma.

Also known as cherry pie, the heliotrope flowers in spring and summer and becomes cloaked in mauve-purple clusters and a far-wafting vanilla aroma, creating swathes of colour as well as fragrance. Originating from South America, these evergreen shrubs have soft-stemmed bushy habits, and usually grow to about 60 cm (2 ft) in height but spread much wider—sensational features in full bloom. Only one species, *Heliotropium arborescens*, is commonly grown but includes popular cultivars such as 'Lord Roberts', with dark purple-green leaves and rich violet flowers, and 'Aureum', which has bright yellow-green leaves and pale lilac blooms.

GROWING NOTES

Heliotropes are best in tropical to temperate gardens, being intolerant of even the lightest frost. The plants prefer full sun and shelter from strong wind, but will also grow in part shade. They require well-drained soil, preferably enriched with organic material, and regular deep watering in warm weather. The plants reach maturity within a few years and can be quite long-lived. Pruning isn't essential, but the shrubs can be lightly trimmed to shape if desired.

HIBISCUS SPECIES & CULTIVARS

HIBISCUS

Hibiscus are great feature shrubs but they can also create exotic screens and informal hedges. Most of the tropical types (above and right) derive from *Hibiscus rosa-sinensis*.

The hibiscus is the archetypal tropical flower—a bloom that evokes thoughts of exotic places wherever it appears. The genus, however, is widely distributed in a range of habitats, including Asia, Africa, Madagascar, North America, the Pacific Islands and Australia, and there are more than 200 species of hibiscus, many with those famous flamboyant blooms.

The Chinese hibiscus, *Hibiscus rosa-sinensis*, is the most influential species, and was distributed by civilisations throughout the Pacific region long before Europeans chartered those waters. It is the floral emblem of Malaysia, but also of Hawaii, where many outstanding forms have been produced. These evergreen shrubs grow 2–4 metres (6–12 ft) in height, and are long-lived but can flower from their first year. In the wild species, which is rarely grown, the flowers are crimson, but in the hundreds of hybrids and cultivars there is an amazing array of colours, as well as double-petalled forms.

Significant, too, is the Syrian rose, *H. syriacus*, which originates in China and India but has been grown in Europe for hundreds of years and is favoured in cooler climates. This

Cultivars of the Syrian rose (opposite) include those with double-petalled flowers. The rose mallow, *Hibiscus moscheutos* (below), is a perennial with enormous blooms.

deciduous species has cultivars with flowers in purple, pink and blue tones, as well as white and bicolours, and some also have contrasting crimson centres or double petals.

GROWING NOTES

Depending on the type, there are *Hibiscus* to suit most garden climates. The Chinese hibiscus is best in tropical to warm areas, while the Syrian rose prefers warm to cold regions. All hibiscus are best in full sun and well-drained soil. Water regularly to establish, after which the plants are very tolerant of drought (although stress will affect their performance). To produce supersized hibiscus blooms, up to 30 cm (12 inches) each in some cultivars, enrich the soil with organic matter and water the plants generously.

HYDRANGEA SPECIES & HYBRIDS
HYDRANGEA

When the hydrangea flowers, it does its best to steal the garden show. The shrub, otherwise fairly benign in appearance, puts on a complicated arrangement of flowers, sterile and fertile, gathered in fancy panicles of dazzling colour, at eye-level of course, to attract our attention.

The most well-known species, *Hydrangea macrophylla*, originates from Japan and was fervently embraced in the 19th century after being introduced to Europe. Early in its cultivation days, it was prized only for its blue flowers (this occurs when some plants are grown in acidic soils containing aluminium). These days, however, we now value its many splendid forms—from flower colours of shocking pink to the softest lilac and shades of white, as well as the lacecap, a variation of the species with a delicate floral style. Many of these hydrangeas are available as potted colour and the dwarfed forms also derive from this species.

Hydrangeas are very easy to grow in gardens as well as containers. *Hydrangea paniculata* (above) is a tall-growing species.

The most commonly grown of these shrubs in gardens is *Hydrangea macrophylla* and its cultivars, including the lacecap variety (right).

Other highly desirable hydrangeas include the oak-leaved hydrangea, *H. quercifolia*, with lobed leaves and a loose flower format, and *H. paniculata*, a lofty shrub that grows to 4 metres (12 ft) or more in height. Both these American species are deciduous and have creamy white blooms.

GROWING NOTES

Hydrangeas grow in many climates, but all enjoy the woodland conditions of their origins: dappled sunlight, rich moist soil and protection from strong wind, sun or heat. Commercially available soil additives can induce the blue flower colour of *H. macrophylla*, but naturally white-flowered hydrangeas are always white. Cut back flowering stems as soon as they have finished, leaving any unflowered growth to produce next year's blooms. Every few years, in winter, remove old stems at ground level to rejuvenate the shrub. The flowers are mostly sterile but hydrangeas are easily propagated by cuttings.

LAVANDULA SPECIES & CULTIVARS
LAVENDER

Ever since the days of the ancient Romans, we've planted lavender in gardens. Although now more ornamental (and commercial) than herbal, the lavenders are indisputable favourites. There are about 30 species of *Lavandula*, most originating around the Mediterranean area, but only a handful are commonly grown. These include *Lavandula dentata*, the so-called French lavender, and the English or common lavender, *L. angustifolia* (syns *L. spica*, *L. officinalis*). Of course, many hybrids and cultivars abound, including those with white, pink and even near-red flowers; the stoechas types that have flowerheads topped with enlarged bracts or 'ears'; and probably the most extensively cultivated of all the lavenders, *L. x intermedia*, the doyen of perfumery.

Depending on the type, lavenders can flower for months in winter, spring or summer. Favoured in gardens are *Lavandula dentata* (right) and the stoechas types (top).

GROWING NOTES
Lavenders grow in climates from warm to cold, but prefer Mediterranean-type conditions. The plants need full sun, open aspects and very well drained soil. Water regularly to establish the plants, after which they are tolerant of dry spells. Cut flowers to prolong the flowering season and to keep the plants tidy; light tip-pruning helps to a maintain compact shape.

LUCULIA GRATISSIMA
LUCULIA

Luculias have clusters of fragrant flowers in autumn and winter. The blooms are usually pink but may also be white.

With their large rounded clusters of delicate pale pink and fragrant flowers, appealingly produced from late autumn throughout winter, luculias are immensely desirable but not always easy to grow. *Luculia gratissima* is an evergreen upright shrub that originates from the Himalayas, but it does not tolerate any frost. The plants are also finicky about garden positions: they must be sheltered from strong wind and partly shaded so their roots are kept cool. In ideal conditions, luculias can live long and grow to more than 3 metres (9 ft) in height, but they are usually smaller in gardens.

GROWING NOTES

Luculias require warm to tropical climates and will not grow in frost-affected cool or temperate areas. They prefer morning sun and also suit dappled shade, although their growth may be sparse. The soil must be well drained and enriched with aged organic matter before planting. Water the plants deeply during spring and summer, and keep their roots cool, but do not allow the soil to become waterlogged. Prune the plants lightly at the end of winter, after flowering.

NERIUM OLEANDER
OLEANDER

The oleander has a reputation as a really tough shrub. It grows in many climates from quite cool to tropical, and withstands strong winds, heavy pollution and front-line coastal conditions. It endures drought, if necessary, for long periods. It isn't fussy about soil and will take harsh pruning. And while oleanders are eminently useful, they are very ornamental too. Evergreen with dense multi-stemmed habits, the species (there's only one in the genus) includes many cultivars: these can mature into tree-like proportions up to 4 metres (20 ft) in height, or they may be dwarf forms less than 1 metre (3 ft) tall. The range of flower colours is extensive and includes double-petal forms. There's also a cultivar with variegated cream and green leaves.

Oleanders flower for months, sometimes from late spring throughout summer and autumn. Flower colours may be white, pink, apricot, crimson or cerise.

GROWING NOTES
Oleanders are very adaptable to most garden climates, except extremely cold conditions. The plants are best in full sun and well-drained soil. Water if necessary during hot, dry weather to ensure good growth and flowering. Be aware that all parts of oleander are poisonous to humans and animals.

PHILADELPHUS SPECIES & CULTIVARS

PHILADELPHUS

The philadelphus or mock orange, as it is sometimes known, has been cultivated for hundreds of years, and although some species, such as the stalwart *Philadelphus coronarius*, remain popular, most of these shrubs in gardens today are cultivars and hybrids—with many of them created when the Asian and North American species met the European ones in the late 19th century. These include the lemon mock orange, *P. x lemoinei*, and its cultivar with double blooms, as well as *P. x virginalis*, which has many forms with extremely fragrant flowers. Most *Philadelphus* in gardens are deciduous and will grow about 2–5 metres (6–15 ft) in height, with dense habits of many arching branches.

Most *Philadelphus* have white or cream flowers in spring and early summer. Many of the hybrids and cultivars have semi-double or double blooms.

GROWING NOTES

These shrubs are best in cool, moist climates, but they will adapt to warmer gardens. They require full sun, or part shade in warm climates. The soil should be well drained and preferably enriched with organic matter. Prune immediately after flowering; in winter, old unproductive canes can be removed to make way for new growth.

The plumbago is easy to grow and will reliably flower for many months, from late spring throughout summer and early autumn.

PLUMBAGO AURICULATA
PLUMBAGO

The heavenly blue flowers of plumbago belie the toughness of these shrubs. An evergreen originating in South Africa, *Plumbago auriculata* is the only species in the genus that is commonly grown. It's a vigorous semi-scrambler that reaches 2–3 metres (6–9 ft) in height, but is very tractable to training and hard pruning. Fast-growing and flowering when young, the plumbago is undemanding in cultivation. The plants can be grown as screens and informal hedges, against walls and fences, and also in pots. Also popular is the white-flowered variety, although this form is less vigorous than the species.

GROWING NOTES
The plumbago will thrive in warm to tropical climates but also suits temperate and cool, frost-free gardens. In cold regions, it may be grown in conservatories. The plants are best in full sun, although they will take some shade. They require well-drained soil, but aren't fussy about quality. Water regularly to establish, after which the plants will tolerate long dry periods. Trim or tip-prune as required to keep the shrubs compact and tidy; heavy pruning should be done in winter.

RAPHIOLEPIS INDICA
INDIAN HAWTHORN

The Indian hawthorn is long-lived but will flower from a young age. The shrub has a naturally compact and dense habit of glossy leaves.

Despite its common name, the Indian hawthorn originates from southern China and it has no thorns. A member of the rose family, this evergreen is known for its delicate fragrant blossoms which cover the shrub in spring. However, it is also much valued for its attractive habit, trouble-free nature and adaptability. Indian hawthorns are densely packed with glossy leaves and usually reach 2–3 metres (6–9 ft) in height. The plants can be grown as screens or clipped into hedges, and will tolerate wind and mild coastal conditions too. *Raphiolepis indica* is the most frequently grown of the genus, but also popular is the hybrid, *R. x delacourii*, with pink flowers.

GROWING NOTES

Indian hawthorns are very adaptable to climates from warm to cool. The plants require full sun to produce the most compact growth, and well-drained, preferably slightly sandy soil. Once established, they will endure mild droughts; however, regular watering throughout spring and summer produces better results. If required, lightly prune after flowering.

ROMNEYA COULTERI
MATILIJA POPPY

With flowers of diaphanous white petals and ruffled yellow centres, and forming a drift of deeply divided blue-green leaves, the matilija poppies are appealing in the garden, but not always easy to grow. *Romneya coulteri*, the only species in cultivation, requires conditions similar to its native habitat of California where it grows in rugged, rocky country and dry riverbeds. The climate has hot dry summers and rainy winters, and the soil is sandy or gravelly and very well drained. Also known as Californian tree poppy, this evergreen shrub, in ideal conditions, can grow to more than 2 metres (6 ft) in height and spreads via suckers. Most *Romneya* in gardens are hybrids or varieties, some with larger-than-usual flowers.

GROWING NOTES
Matilija poppies grow in climates from cool to warm, but do prefer conditions that replicate their homeland. The plants need full sun all day. They don't like clay soils, high humidity or summer rain. Remove flowers as they finish to keep the shrubs tidy, and, because the plants bloom on new growth, cut back the stems to ground level in winter.

The matilija poppy flowers from spring to summer, depending on the climate. The blooms have petals like silk, and are fragrant.

RONDELETIA AMOENA
RONDELETIA

Even though there are about 120 species in the genus *Rondeletia*, few are commonly grown in gardens. This is mainly because these evergreen shrubs, native to Mexico, South America and the West Indies, are extremely frost tender, but is also due to the outstanding popularity of one species. *Rondeletia amoena* is the most ornamental of these plants in gardens. It is long-lived, eventually growing to about 3 metres (9 ft) in height after several years, but flowers from a young age. In late winter and spring, the shrub is covered in huge trusses of fragrant, red-budded, pale pink flowers, borne in such profusion that the arching branches bow graciously with the weight of their glory.

The rondeletia forms a spreading crown of fine arching branches that bear profuse clusters of fragrant blooms in late winter and spring.

GROWING NOTES

Rondeletias require warm to tropical, frost-free climates. They are best in full sun, with shelter from strong or cold wind. The plants prefer well-drained soil that is heavily enriched with aged organic matter. They need regular watering throughout the warmer seasons, but should be kept fairly dry in winter. Prune after flowering to keep plants compact; in mature shrubs, the oldest canes can be removed at ground level.

A new age of roses has dawned, with easy-care forms for modern gardens. These include shrub types like 'Buff Beauty' (below), groundcover roses (right), and miniatures such as 'Marilyn' (opposite).

ROSA SPECIES & CULTIVARS
ROSE

From ancient times to the gardens of today, the rose has inspired more devotion than any other plant. Everyone loves a rose, and those who don't simply haven't met the right one. From the species, or wild roses, and the heritage forms to the 'modern' hybrid tea, created in the 19th century, and the new-age types such as the miniatures, groundcovers, floribundas and David Austins, there are now many thousands of roses for gardens and gardeners.

Rose-lovers hold that plant type is irrelevant—what is important is the rose. Gardeners should take note and simply choose the plants that best suit their needs and the flowers they like most. Those who get hooked should join a society; talk to other growers; read books about roses; and, most importantly, seek out specialist nurseries who supply top-of-the-range plants—a rose can be a lifetime commitment so it's wise to start with the best.

There are thousands of rose cultivars for gardeners to choose from, as well as many wild roses like *Rosa banksiae* (above) and *R. laevigata* (below).

GROWING NOTES

Roses will grow in climates from tropical to cold, depending on the plant type. They prefer full sun all day for maximum growth and flowering, and well-drained soil that is heavily enriched with aged organic matter before planting. The plants need good air circulation; however, very strong wind will ruin the flowers. Regular feeding promotes prolific plants, but most roses will flower anyway. Pruning depends on the type of rose—some require traditional-style pruning, usually in late winter or early spring, while others can be simply trimmed at any time by removing the finished flowers and dead stems. Pests and diseases must be controlled for roses to perform at their best, but in recent years rose breeders have concentrated on improving the plants' resistance to these problems.

SPIRAEA SPECIES & CULTIVARS
SPIRAEA

S ometimes known as bridal wreath or may bush, spiraeas are deciduous shrubs renowned for their spring flower displays that are like floating clouds of tiny blossoms. Many of the ornamental species, originating mainly from China and Japan, have white flowers, like the well-known *Spiraea cantoniensis* and its double-flowered forms. However, there are also some spiraeas with pink blooms, such as *S. japonica*, along with numerous hybrids and cultivars. Most of the spiraeas grow about 1–3 metres (3–9 ft) in height, and have rounded habits of slender arching stems, as well as fine leaves with attractive autumn colours.

GROWING NOTES

Spiraeas grow in climates from warm to cool, but are best in cool, moist regions. They require full sun and well-drained soil. Water regularly to establish, after which spiraeas are tolerant of dry periods. Avoid heavy-handed pruning, which spoils the plant's natural shape; if desired, trim lightly after flowering. With mature plants, the old, unproductive canes can be removed at ground level to make way for new growth.

Spiraeas are long-lived, and while it takes several years to get the full effect of frothy blooms, the plants will start flowering when young.

TETRADENIA RIPARIA
MISTY PLUME BUSH

T here are only five species in this genus from tropical and southern Africa, and just one in common cultivation. *Tetradenia riparia* (syn. *Iboza riparia*) is also known as the musk bush or nutmeg bush for its aromatic foliage, but its trademark asset in gardens is its feathery plumes of flowers. Minute but massed on sprays about 30 cm (1 ft) long, the blooms crown the shrub for weeks in winter. For the rest of the year, the misty plume bush is still a pleasure to have around in the garden, with its velvety grey-green leaves that freely release their fragrance if touched.

GROWING NOTES

The misty plume bush is best in warm to tropical climates. In cooler regions, it may be grown in pots in sheltered situations. The plants require full sun and protection from strong wind. They like well-drained soil, but aren't choosy about the type. Long-lived but flowering young, these semi-evergreen shrubs grow to 2 metres (6 ft) in height and almost as wide. Prune after flowering to promote a compact shape and new growth.

The flowers of the misty plume bush may be mauve, pink or white, depending on the variety. Its fragrant leaves are also appealing.

IBOZA RIPARIA
Eastern & Southern Africa
Family: Lamiaceae
Order: Lamiales

VIBURNUM SPECIES & CULTIVARS
VIBURNUM

Treasures of the cottage garden and the romantic woodland, the viburnums are often classed among the old-fashioned favourites, and deservedly so, for their timeless beauty has enchanted gardeners for centuries. Viburnums are renowned for their voluptuous flowerheads, mostly pure white and sweetly scented; however, the genus is known for other charms. There are deciduous species that have attractive autumn foliage, and evergreens with glossy leaves that make fine hedges; many forms feature clusters of bright red, winter berries, and viburnums are easy to grow as well.

There are about 150 species of *Viburnum*, originating in Asia and North America. Many of these are ornamental and there are also several hybrids and cultivars. These include famous flowering forms, such as the guelder rose, *Viburnum opulus*, the Chinese snowball tree, *V. macrocephalum*, and the hybrids, like *V. x burkwoodii*, which can have white flowers that are tinged

Viburnums are easy to grow in various garden styles, from romantic designs or borders to hedges and pots: guelder rose (above); Chinese snowball tree (right).

with red or pink. Also popular is the laurustinus, *V. tinus*, an evergreen species from the Mediterranean region which has blooms throughout winter and early spring but is favoured in hedging for its naturally dense foliage.

GROWING NOTES

Most viburnums prefer temperate to cool climates, although some will also grow in warm or subtropical gardens. In cool gardens, the plants are best in full sun, but they require part shade in warmer situations. The soil should be well drained and enriched with aged organic matter. Protection from strong wind is preferred, especially for viburnums with heavy panicles of large blooms. Water the plants generously in spring and summer. Viburnums can vary in height from 1 to 4 metres (3–12 ft) and are long-lived, but will flower within a few years.

Most viburnums, such as *Viburnum x burkwoodii* (left) and *V. plicatum* (above), are featured for their spring flowerheads but these shrubs can also have decorative foliage and berries.

WEIGELA FLORIDA & CULTIVARS
WEIGELA

Weigela florida flowers throughout spring and sometimes early summer. The fine, arching branches bear clusters of tubular blooms in tones of pink.

Festooned with flared bell-shaped flowers, in delicate shades of pink from blushing white to rosy hues, the weigelas look dainty in gardens but are very adaptable and easy to grow. This genus of deciduous shrubs originates from Japan, Korea and China, and the popular species *Weigela florida* has many cultivars including the red-flowered 'Eva Rathke', 'Candida', with white blooms, and 'Variegata', which has pale pink flowers and green and creamy-white leaves. Deciduous shrubs, weigelas will grow 2–3 metres (6–9 ft) in height and develop multi-stemmed habits of slender, arching branches that become dense with leaves and flowers in spring.

GROWING NOTES

Weigelas grow in most garden climates, except for dry or tropical regions. They require full sun and protection from strong wind. The plants appreciate organically enriched soil and mulching. Every few years, prune the oldest canes to ground level to rejuvenate the plant and make way for new growth. Avoid trimming the tips of branches as this detracts from their graceful, arching form.

rhododendron & azalea

The rhododendron is more than a flowering shrub, it is a flowering prize. There are gardens devoted to the plants; they have inspired specialist growers and societies; shows are held to honour them; and some gardeners have even dedicated their lifetimes to the cultivation of *Rhododendron*—the 'rose tree'.

The rhododendron's popularity is especially phenomenal considering the plant's fairly short cultivation history. Although there are about 900 species in the genus *Rhododendron*, distributed mostly throughout Asia but also elsewhere in the northern hemisphere, the first of these only trickled into mainstream horticulture a few hundred years ago. However, by the late 1800s, the trickle had become a flood, as the rhododendrons were targeted by a flurry of plant collectors and hybridisers alike, and 'rhodo-fever' has gripped gardeners ever since.

Now, there are more than 9,000 named cultivars of *Rhododendron*—the botanical name means 'rose tree'. This horticultural feat has caused the genus to split into three coalitions, and among gardeners the plants are commonly known as the rhododendrons, the vireyas and the azaleas.

The rhododendrons, also called broad-leaf rhododendrons, are mostly evergreen and large, up to 4 metres (12 ft) in height. The group is renowned for flowers in flamboyant trusses, from late winter to spring. It includes many species and cultivars, with an extensive range of flower colours—pink, red, mauve, purple, orange, yellow, white or cream—and some are fragrant too. The blooms also vary in form—with single, semi-double and double petals, as well as the 'hose-in-hose' types, where one flower appears to be placed inside another.

Rhododendrons, azaleas and vireyas all belong to the genus *Rhododendron*. The vireyas (opposite) have typically elegant flower clusters in warm colours.

Once established, a garden featuring azaleas and rhododendrons is very low maintenance. These mostly evergreen shrubs will flower flamboyantly, but also add year-round foliage and structure to garden designs.

The vireyas are the tropical members of the genus, and are quite similar in appearance to the rhododendrons. Evergreen shrubs, rarely growing more than 2 metres (6 ft) in height, vireyas are known for their glossy leaves and clusters of large, tubular flowers. Although some species of vireyas are grown, the cultivars are more popular—most have flower colours in warm tones, from creamy-white or soft yellow and apricot to rosy-pink and red. Between them, the vireyas have a long flowering season, from late summer to early winter, but individual plants can also flower more than once each year.

Azaleas used to be classed as a separate genus, but are now recognised as another of *Rhododendron*'s disguises. With variable habits, from less than 60 cm (2 ft) in height to more than 2 metres (6 ft) tall, the azaleas themselves have become so numerous that they are divided into subgroups. The Mollis type is distinguished within the group and genus for being deciduous, and these plants usually have flowers in cream, yellow, orange or red tones. The evergreen Indica azaleas are among the rhododendron's most popular forms, with flowers that are predominantly pink, purple and red or white, sometimes in combinations of colours, or with frilled, ruffled or double petals. The Kurume azaleas, originally raised in Japan, are especially valued for their dainty leaves and habits that become covered in mostly pink or purple blooms.

Azaleas (opposite) have a diverse range of growing habits as well as flower forms, and they are very adaptable. They thrive in pots and some can even be clipped into hedges. Most of the azaleas flower in late winter and spring.

GROWING NOTES

With so many forms of *Rhododendron* in cultivation, there are plants to suit most garden climates and styles. Many of the ancestral species originate in mountainous, woodland habitats and prefer those conditions. The rhododendrons and Mollis azaleas, in particular, are best in cool to cold climates. The Indica and Kurume azaleas are more adaptable, and grow in climates from warm to cool, with the Kurumes being more tolerant of cold. Vireyas suit climates from tropical to cool; they prefer high humidity and must be protected from frost.

In general, all rhododendrons and azaleas prefer partly shaded conditions, such as dappled light or morning sun only, and shelter from strong wind. There are, however, many cultivars which adapt to full sun. The soil must be well drained and enriched with organic matter. Rhododendrons are famous for their love of acidic soils, and azaleas especially will languish in the presence of lime. Water the plants regularly, especially in spring and summer, or during dry, windy weather. Many of the azaleas and vireyas are easily grown in pots, and can also be brought indoors while flowering to grace our homes.

Rhododendrons and azaleas are widely available, and best obtained in flower so you know exactly what you're getting. For top-shelf types, seek specialist growers and nurseries who can supply great plants as well as advice on caring for them.

Rhododendrons, vireyas and azaleas can be featured in many garden styles, and are ideal for wild woodlands, mixed shrubberies and sweeping borders.

foliage
shrubs

Foliage shrubs are grown for their leaves, whether evergreen and brilliant throughout the seasons, brightly toned when fresh in spring, or deciduous and rich in autumn colour. Their beauty lies simply in their leaves and habits, even though many will also flower. Foliage shrubs provide structure and permanence but they also bring a sense of verdancy to the garden year round.

Foliage shrubs can create a living tapestry with shades of green, colour contrasts, variegations and seasonal tones. This page: A hedge of pittosporum, strawberry trees and holly. Previous pages: *Helichrysum petiolare* 'Limelight'.

There are many trees and shrubs that have ornamental foliage as well as assets like fruit or flowers, and some of these have been included in other chapters of this book. In this chapter, we feature shrubs that have become famous mainly for their outstanding leaf colours or forms, but also plants which are often used in knots, hedges and topiary—ancient arts of foliage in the garden.

Foliage shrubs provide enduring forms in garden designs and they also have ornamental charms in all the seasons. Left: Pittosporum and photinia hedge. Right: Pittosporum. Following pages: Foliage design with junipers and maples.

ACALYPHA WILKESIANA
FIJIAN FIRE PLANT

The Fijian fire plant has leaves that are large, glossy, perfectly ovate and brilliantly coloured. In warm gardens, these shrubs are fast-growing and long-lived.

The leaves of the Fijian fire plant are among the most remarkably coloured in nature, making this shrub a spectacular feature all year round. In the species, which is not only from Fiji but also other Pacific Islands, the leaves are darkest burgundy and bronze to bright green, with wide red margins. But there are cultivars galore, and these include forms with striking leaf variegations of lucent yellow and lime, green edged with cream, or pink splashed with green. Most Fijian fire plants grow into dense bushes 2–3 metres (6–9 ft) in height, with a similar spread. Their brilliant appearance always makes an impact in the garden, whether grown in borders, as accents, in large pots or as informal hedges.

GROWING NOTES

Acalypha wilkesiana and its cultivars suit warm, frost-free gardens and are ideal for tropical and subtropical climates. In cooler areas, they must be wintered in glasshouses. The foliage of the plants is best in full sun, but they will take slight shade. Water regularly during warmer seasons.

ARTEMISIA SPECIES & CULTIVARS

WORMWOOD

Although their medicinal qualities have been known since the days of the ancient Egyptians, wormwoods are now more valued in gardens for their foliage—grey-green, silvery or near white, and feathered, fern-like or lacy. Forming rounded billowing clumps about 1 metre (3 ft) high and wide, these evergreen shrubs have become indispensable to neutral-coloured designs or those which feature foliage highlights, as well as herb gardens. While the species, such as the French tarragon, *Artemisia dracunculus*, of culinary fame, and the southernwood, *A. abrotanum*, remain popular, the cultivars are favoured ornamentally. These include 'Lambrook Silver' and 'Powis Castle', both with very decorative leaves.

The soft silvery leaves of wormwood are easy to place in a variety of garden designs, from mixed borders and herb gardens to informal hedging.

GROWING NOTES

Wormwoods are easy to grow in climates from warm to cool, although they won't suit the tropics. They tolerate frost, as well as coastal conditions. These shrubs require full sun and good air circulation. The soil must be well drained, but may be poor quality. Water regularly to establish, after which the plants will withstand drought. Wormwoods can be short-lived, but may be propagated from cuttings.

AUCUBA JAPONICA CULTIVARS
JAPANESE LAUREL

Variegated forms of the Japanese laurel include *Aucuba japonica* var. *variegata* (right), and 'Crotonifolia' (below).

While the Japanese laurel, *Aucuba japonica*, is a handsome shrub with large, thick, glossy green leaves, its cultivars have far more exciting foliage. These include variegated forms with foliage that is spotted, speckled or streaked with gold, silver or shiny white, such as the gold dust plant, *A. japonica* var. *variegata*; as well as a variety with deeply serrated, dark green leaves. All the Japanese laurels are evergreen, and fairly slow-growing, but eventually form rounded shrubs about 3 metres (9 ft) in height. They have naturally neat and dense habits which suit informal hedges, screening and woodland-style shrubberies, and will also grow in containers or indoors.

GROWING NOTES

The Japanese laurels will grow in cool to warm climates, but prefer mild, moist environments. They are best in dappled shade or with morning sun only; the variegated-leaf forms being especially susceptible to sunburn. The soil should be well drained but moist, and enriched for good growth. The shrubs may also produce bright red berries, if both male and female types are planted.

BERBERIS SPECIES & CULTIVARS
BARBERRY

The barberries form a huge group of more than 450 species which are distributed throughout Asia, Europe and the Americas, yet few of the genus are commonly grown. This is partly due to wheat rust, a dreaded disease which some species of barberry will harbour, outlawing them in wheat-growing areas, but also because the ornamental forms of *Berberis* have been outstandingly successful.

The ornamental barberries are attractive year round and versatile in garden designs. Most are deciduous, with small rounded leaves that turn brilliant red in autumn. The shrubs are sprinkled with flowers in spring, and their arching branches are hung with colourful berries throughout autumn and winter. Traditionally used in hedges because their stems are profusely spiny, barberries can also be featured unclipped and allowed to develop their natural billowing forms.

Many barberry species are common in cultivation, including the evergreen *Berberis darwinii*, which was first collected from South America by Charles Darwin on his famous *Beagle* trip.

The most commonly grown barberry, *Berberis thunbergii* (left), has popular cultivars featuring colourful foliage of red tones or yellow, such as 'Aurea' (above).

Most barberries have naturally attractive arching habits, with fine spiny stems and small rounded leaves; these shrubs are also long-lived.

However, the most popular is *B. thunbergii*, a deciduous shrub about 1 metre (3 ft) high and wide, and its cultivars. These include 'Atropurpurea', which has burgundy foliage that turns crimson in autumn, the dwarf form 'Atropurpurea Nana', and 'Aurea' with golden-yellow leaves.

GROWING NOTES

Most of the ornamental barberries are best in cool climates, but also grow in warmer regions. They prefer full sun all day, and the coloured-leaf cultivars are disappointing without it. The plants grow in a range of soil types, but are best in well-drained, enriched conditions. Water regularly to establish and to promote good growth; however, these plants are also quite tolerant of drought. If required, prune the shrubs in winter; hedges may be lightly trimmed as required.

BUXUS SPECIES & CULTIVARS
BOX

Cultivated for thousands of years, the common box, *Buxus sempervirens*, is one of the most influential plants in gardening.

The indisputable king of foliage plants, box has been in gardens since gardens, as we know them, began. It is synonymous with hedges and topiary, and was among the first subjects of these arts. From ancient Roman times and Pliny the Younger (62–110 BCE), who was very keen on whimsical box shapes, through the extravagant Renaissance with its topiaried everything, to knots and parterres and the minimalist styles of today, box has become part of gardening.

The common box, *Buxus sempervirens*, is immeasurably influential, and is the definitive evergreen shrub of hedging, topiary and formal designs. Although the wild species grows about 8 metres (24 ft) in height, it is rarely left to its own devices. The common box also has many cultivars, including a variegated form with white-edged leaves and dwarf varieties that are ideal for mini-hedges.

Also very popular is the Japanese box, *B. microphylla* var. *japonica*, which grows 1–2 metres (3–6 ft) tall, has rounded, pale green leaves, and is more suitable for warmer climates.

GROWING NOTES

All forms of box are evergreen, slow-growing and very long-lived. They prefer cool to cold climates, although the Japanese box adapts well to more temperate regions. The plants are versatile in gardens, and they can also be grown (and shaped) in pots. Although very adaptable, they are best in full sun and well-drained soil. For plants in containers, hedging and topiary, soil enriched with organic matter and regular watering will promote strong growth. Box will flower in spring, but despite being lightly scented the blooms are fairly insignificant. To shape the plants, clip with shears as required.

Box is both adaptable and versatile. These plants can bring formality and a sense of classic grace to garden designs, but also a touch of whimsy.

CODIAEUM VARIEGATUM VAR. *PICTUM*
CROTON

Few shrubs can claim foliage colour as exciting as the crotons—which offer a variegated feast of leaves in gold, yellow, orange, red, crimson, pink and white; often splashed, striped or spotted. The leaf shapes of crotons vary, too: these may be straight-edged, wavy or lobed; broad ovate or long and narrow; even twisted. All these cultivars derive from just one variety of one species, *Codiaeum variegatum* var. *pictum*, which originates in the Pacific Islands and Malaysia. In tropical gardens, crotons can be used to create dazzling drifts, hedges or shrubberies, and may grow 1–2 metres (3–6 ft) tall. However, they also make colourful pot plants, for sunny courtyards and balconies as well as indoors.

The many colourful cultivars of croton are easy to grow in tropical-style gardens, but also in pots and indoors.

GROWING NOTES
Crotons are best in tropical and subtropical climates. In gardens, the plants need full sun to obtain their best colour (though they will grow in part shade), and protection from strong wind. Indoors, crotons require bright, warm positions. The soil must be well drained and enriched with organic matter. Water generously during the growing season.

The mirror bush (above) is very adaptable to garden styles and climates. *Coprosma* x *kirkii* (right) is a low-growing hybrid.

COPROSMA REPENS
MIRROR BUSH

I t's easy to see how this coprosma gets its common name of mirror bush—its leaves are super-shiny. These evergreen shrubs make great glossy hedges or foliage features, and are densely packed with ovate leaves that are rich green in the species, but may be variegated with silver, gold or cream in cultivars. There's also a popular hybrid, *Coprosma* x *kirkii*, which is often used as a spreading groundcover and only grows 30–60 cm (1–2 ft) in height. All mirror bushes are low-maintenance, fast-growing and long-lived, and they are easily clipped to shape as well.

GROWING NOTES
Most types of *Coprosma* will grow in a range of climates from tropical to cool. They are very tolerant of coastal conditions, dry seasons, strong winds and light frost; and they also adapt well to inhospitable urban conditions, such as exposed balconies or rooftops. The plants are best in full sun, which encourages dense growth, and must have well-drained soil. Shaping and tip-pruning can be performed year round, with heavier pruning in early winter or late spring.

CORDYLINE FRUTICOSA
TI

The cordylines form an intriguing group of plants which belongs to the same family as agaves and other such succulents, but also includes the prehistoric-looking cabbage trees of Australia and New Zealand. Their best-known form, however, is the ti, *Cordyline fruticosa* (syn. *C. terminalis*), also known as the Hawaiian good luck plant—with its many cultivars that have exotically coloured leaves of glossy green, red, pink, purple, yellow and white, often surreally striped. Native to tropical eastern Asia and Polynesia, tis are popular in warm-climate gardens, and can be used to create exciting foliage effects and hedges, but they are also commonly grown in pots and indoors.

Tis have many varieties with exciting foliage colours, including striped leaves. These shrubs are ideal for shady gardens and indoor displays.

GROWING NOTES

Tis are best in tropical, subtropical and warm gardens. In cooler climates, they are grown indoors. These evergreen shrubs can reach 3 metres (9 ft) in height and will spread, via suckers, into dramatic clumps; but they are usually much smaller in containers. They grow in full sun or part shade, and prefer well-drained soil that is heavily enriched. Water regularly in spring and summer, less in winter.

COTINUS SPECIES & CULTIVARS
SMOKE BUSH

The smoke bush, *Cotinus coggygria*, which originates in limited pockets of Europe and Asia, is botanically uncommon, with only one other species, the American smoke tree, *C. obovatus*, in the genus. Although these species get their common names from their distinctive plumes of tiny massed flowers which are pale pink and age to purple-grey, they are also renowned in gardens for their deciduous autumn foliage of red, purple, orange and yellow tones. The smoke bush has cultivars with colourful spring and summer foliage as well, including some with dark purple or burgundy leaves.

GROWING NOTES

The smoke bush prefers cool to cold climates, and is tolerant of frost; however, it will also grow in warmer gardens. The plants are best in full sun, especially the coloured-leaf cultivars. They require well-drained, fairly rich soil, and protection from strong wind. The smoke bush grows about 3–5 metres (9–15 ft) in height and has a spreading habit that enhances its billowing display. If required, mature shrubs can be pruned in winter.

The smoke bush features plumes of flowers followed by colourful autumn leaves. Cultivars may have burgundy or purple foliage in spring and summer.

ELAEAGNUS PUNGENS
JAPANESE OLEASTER

Evergreen and easy to grow, the Japanese oleaster has long been valued in landscaping as a dependable shrub or hedging plant. Its shiny ovate leaves are wavy-edged with characteristic brown dots on the silvery undersides, and the foliage is densely packed in a slightly spiny, multi-branched habit, to about 3 metres (9 ft) in height. The shrub also has clusters of fragrant cream flowers in summer, followed by berries that ripen red in autumn. Even more popular, however, are the variegated cultivars—some with yellow leaves splashed green, others with glossy green leaves edged in gold. These have all the features of the species but also provide year-round foliage colour and make outstanding hedges.

Variegated forms of Japanese oleaster are easy to grow and also provide outstanding foliage colour year round.

GROWING NOTES

Most types of Japanese oleaster are very adaptable to climates from warm to cold. They will tolerate heavy frost and coastal conditions, but dislike tropical climates. The plants prefer full sun, especially the variegated cultivars, and well-drained soil. If required, prune lightly in spring to maintain a compact shape and keep the plant tidy; trim hedges as required.

The most popular spindle trees are the variegated forms of *Euonymus japonicus*; yellow-leaved cultivars make outstanding hedges of gold.

EUONYMUS JAPONICUS
SPINDLE TREE

The wild forms of *Euonymus japonicus*, a species that originates in China and Japan, are valued for their glossy green, rounded foliage, but in gardens these shrubs are more frequently grown for their variegated leaves. Selective cultivation over centuries has produced a vast array of these ornamental forms—some have leaves with fine creamy margins or wide white edges, others are marked with yellow patches or splashed with gold. There are also cultivars with streaky stems or brightly coloured new growth.

The spindle trees are evergreen and long-lived, with dense habits that make them very suitable for hedging—the coloured-leaf forms are especially spectacular when used in this way. However, they are also ideal as feature shrubs in foliage-based designs and mixed borders. Spindle trees are naturally neat and compact, growing 3–4 metres (9–12 ft) in height and 2 metres (6 ft) wide at maturity, and, if unclipped, they require very little maintenance.

Spindle trees are low-maintenance and suit many designs, from hedging to mixed borders. The species has glossy green leaves, but cultivars may have foliage tones of gold and silver.

GROWING NOTES

These evergreen shrubs will adapt to various climates from warm to cool. They also tolerate frost and coastal conditions. Spindle trees require full sun, and the variegated types will not develop their best colours without it. The soil should be well drained, and preferably enriched with organic matter, especially in hedges. Water regularly to establish the plants, after which they will withstand dry periods; however, the stress of drought does slow their growth. Even in hedges, the spindle trees don't need a lot of trimming: lightly clip to shape as required throughout the year, and prune back in winter if necessary. These shrubs can be planted closely, at 60 cm (2 ft) intervals, to promote fast-forming hedges.

HELICHRYSUM SPECIES & CULTIVARS
HELICHRYSUM

Helichrysums with outstanding leaves include the species *Helichrysum basalticum* (above) and the cultivar of *H. petiolare* 'Limelight' (right).

Although they hail from an extensive family of flowering annuals and perennials that includes everlasting daisies, these helichrysums are grown for their foliage. They have wonderful leaves—soft to look at and to touch, in a range of light-reflecting colours. In the species *Helichrysum petiolare*, the foliage is silvery grey-green, but one of its best cultivars is 'Limelight', with luminous yellow-green leaves. These helichrysums have lovely habits, too, forming billowing mounds about 1.5 metres (5 ft) in height and 2 metres (6 ft) wide. Depending on the design situation, they can be trimmed to shape but they may also trail in a relaxed, sprawling manner that is ideal for cascading over walls or in containers.

GROWING NOTES

These shrub-style helichrysums grow in climates from warm to cool; they tolerate temperatures down to freezing, but not frost. The plants are best in light shade or morning sun only. The soil should be well drained, but enriched with aged organic matter. Do not overwater, and avoid watering from above, if possible, as it can spoil the foliage.

JUNIPERUS SPECIES & CULTIVARS
JUNIPER

Junipers are the reigning ornamentals of the conifer dynasty. They have distinctive cones or 'berries' that decorate the plants for many seasons.

The most popular of all the great conifers in gardens, junipers have been cultivated for centuries—in China, Japan, Europe, North America and throughout the northern hemisphere, where they are naturally found from the highest mountain ranges to the tropics. Famously, there's the common juniper, *Juniperus communis*, and its berries used for culinary and medicinal purposes and for gin. However, in the genus *Juniperus* there are about 60 species and many of these are ornamentally grown. They also have numerous varieties and cultivars—amounting to hundreds of types of juniper, for all kinds of gardens and styles.

Junipers are distinguished from other conifers by their unusual cones, which are fleshy and fruit-like. And while all junipers have these 'berries', their range of habits is remarkably diverse. There are trees and shrubs and prostrate forms, and they vary in height from 60 cm (2 ft) to 20 metres (60 ft) tall,

and in habit from conical or columnar to rounded or groundcovering. There's also a great variety of foliage forms, including fine needles, fanned shapes and even twisted leaves, as well as a range of colours, from grey-green or steel blue to bronze or yellow-gold.

GROWING NOTES

With the many junipers available, there are plants to suit garden climates from cold to tropical; however, most grow best in cool to warm regions. Junipers, in general, require full sun and very well drained soil. Some species will tolerate strong wind and front-line coastal situations, while others will adapt to dry conditions. The plants rarely need trimming, although they can be lightly clipped to keep them compact and shapely. Many junipers will also grow in pots, and they have long been favoured subjects of bonsai.

Unlike many conifers, which dominate a garden's style, junipers are very versatile. They include shrubs which can be clipped into hedges and prostrate species, such as *Juniperus conferta* (above).

LIGUSTRUM OVALIFOLIUM 'AUREUM'
GOLDEN PRIVET

E ven though it belongs to a prolific group of trees and shrubs that is infamous for invasive tendencies, the golden privet is an ornamental favourite, especially for the creation of outstandingly coloured hedges. The golden privet is a cultivar, 'Aureum', of a Japanese species, with variegated leaves that may be gold and green or almost entirely bright yellow. Unpruned as a specimen shrub, this evergreen can grow to 4 metres (12 ft) in height, but it is often seen as a hedge about 1–2 metres (3–6 ft) tall. Like all privets, this golden form is very easy to grow; but you must remove any plain green foliage as it can take over.

GROWING NOTES
Golden privets are very adaptable to a wide range of conditions, though are best in warm to tropical climates. They must have full sun all day to maintain dense growth and the golden foliage colour. The soil should be well drained, but not necessarily rich. Once established, the plants are tolerant of drought. Shear off the flowers to prevent fruits from setting.

The golden privets are fast-growing and easy to care for; they are often trimmed into spectacular specimens or hedges, but privets do flower as well.

MELIANTHUS MAJOR
HONEYBUSH

The honeybush produces striking flower spikes in summer, but these shrubs are more often cultivated for their unusual leaves.

Native to South Africa, the honeybush may be named for its nectar-filled flowers which are burgundy-red and strikingly borne on tall spikes, but most gardeners grow this plant for its leaves. With rare blue-grey tones, the honeybush leaf can be more than 30 cm (1 ft) long and is composed of many toothed leaflets—like a frond of some surreal fern. Evergreen, these shrubs can grow more than 2 metres (6 ft) in height and often wider, spreading by suckers into formidable clumps. *Melianthus major* is botanically, as well as visually, unusual, with only one cultivated species in the genus.

GROWING NOTES
The honeybush is best in tropical to temperate climates. It will grow in cooler gardens, but the leaves will be destroyed by frost and the plant's crown and roots must be protected over winter in order for it to regenerate in spring. The plants require full sun and well-drained soil that is enriched, for good foliage growth. While established plants will tolerate mild periods of drought, they provide better displays when watered regularly in spring and summer.

MYRTUS COMMUNIS
MYRTLE

For centuries, the myrtle has been favoured in hedges; but left unclipped, the plant will produce fragrant, white fluffy flowers in spring, followed by blue-black berries.

Many hundreds of plants are generally called myrtles; however, there are only two species in the genus which gives its name to this great family, Myrtaceae. *Myrtus communis*, the common myrtle, is the archetype. Although it is also called the English myrtle (because it is so widely grown in the United Kingdom), the species originates from the Mediterranean region. Here, the myrtle has been honoured since Classical days when it was first made into wreaths, medicine, perfume and spice, but it was also grown in ancient gardens, clipped into elegant hedges—a tradition that continues today.

GROWING NOTES

Myrtles grow in most garden climates, except the tropics or extreme cold. The plants are best in full sun, which produces compact foliage, but tolerate some shade. The soil should be well drained, and enriched to promote growth. Myrtles are evergreen, growing about 3 metres (9 ft) in height and width, and are densely packed with glossy leaves. Prune after flowering to keep growth compact; if hedging, clip several times during the growing season.

NANDINA DOMESTICA
SACRED BAMBOO

With evergreen leaves that turn flaming red as the weather cools, followed by clusters of shiny crimson berries, sacred bamboo is one of the most versatile ornamental shrubs for gardens. From public landscapes to intimate courtyards and Oriental styles or pots, *Nandina domestica* suits many designs. It is nearly indestructible, too. Despite its common name, sacred bamboo is not related to bamboo but is part of the berberis family. There is only one species in this genus from China, and this grows 1.5–2 metres (5–6 ft) in height; however, its popularity has ensured that several cultivars are available. These include 'Nana', which has a low-growing habit, and 'Alba', a rarer, white-berried form.

GROWING NOTES

Sacred bamboo grows in most garden climates, except the tropics, in full sun or part shade. The flowers are insignificant, appearing in summer and early autumn. Plants do tolerate dry periods but grow and look better if watered regularly. They are often used as informal hedges or screening plants, but avoid strict clipping as this spoils their natural shape.

The leaves of sacred bamboo turn red in cool weather, providing a colour display that's long-lasting. Autumn and winter berries are an additional highlight.

PHOTINIA SPECIES & CULTIVARS
PHOTINIA

Photinias make great hedges. Unclipped, the plants will produce panicles of spring flowers.

Although there are about 60 species of photinia, all from eastern Asia, the genus is best-known for its evergreen forms that have remarkably colourful new leaves. From bronze or bright red to almost pink, the fresh growth of these photinias is easily exploited by regular trimming. They create flamboyant foliage features in the garden all year round but are also famed for transforming hedges into works of art.

The most commonly grown of these colourful cultivars includes the red-leafed photinia, *Photinia glabra* 'Rubens', which has brilliant crimson new foliage; the Chinese hawthorn, *P. serrulata*, with serrated leaves; and the fast-growing hybrid, *P.* x *fraseri* 'Robusta'. Unpruned, these evergreen shrubs will reach 5–7 metres (15–21 ft) in height, with naturally dense and rounded habits, but they are often clipped in hedges 2–3 metres (6–9 ft) tall. Most also have decorative clusters of creamy-white flowers, and although they are rarely seen on strictly clipped photinias, the blooms are an added feature when the plants are informally grown.

GROWING NOTES

These coloured-leaf photinias prefer cool climates but they will also adapt to warmer gardens. They need full sun to develop their best foliage tones, and to keep the plants growing densely in hedges. The soil must be well drained; photinias have few problems except root rot in waterlogged conditions. The plants require regular watering in spring and summer, especially in dry seasons; be especially generous with those in hedges. The coloured-leaf photinias can be lightly and frequently trimmed to encourage new growth year round. Structural pruning, if required, should be done in late winter.

The flowers of photinias are followed by decorative berries. *Photinia glabra* 'Rubens' (above) is one of the most popular forms for hedging.

PIERIS SPECIES & CULTIVARS
PIERIS

Often known as lily-of-the-valley tree for its sprays of creamy-white bell-shaped flowers, pieris is also ornamentally valued for its spectacularly coloured new growth. In some species, such as *Pieris japonica*, *P. formosa* and *P. forrestii*, the young spring leaves are dazzling red or intensely pink. They rival the profuse display of flowers and stand out against the older, dark green leaves. *Pieris japonica* grows to about 2–3 metres (6–9 ft) in height, and has a sprawling habit, but can also be grown in pots. It has many cultivars which vary in flower colour, from dark pink to white and sometimes a combination of both, as well as a variegated foliage form with green leaves edged in cream.

Many *Pieris* feature brilliantly coloured new leaves, but they also have sprays of bell-shaped flowers. These shrubs can be used in hedges.

GROWING NOTES

These evergreen shrubs prefer cool, moist climates but will adapt to warmer areas. They require sheltered, partly shaded positions that are protected from hot sun and strong wind. The soil should be well drained but enriched with aged organic matter. In these conditions, the shrubs are long-lived and produce their best flowers and leaf colour.

PITTOSPORUM

The pittosporums are an extensive group of evergreen trees and shrubs, with more than 200 species distributed in Asia, South Africa, Australia, New Zealand and Hawaii. Between them, they have a swag of attractions, including fragrant flowers, like the Japanese mock orange, *Pittosporum tobira*, or decorative berries, such as those of *P. rhombifolium*, which are bright yellow, orange or red and long-lasting. However, many pittosporum species, such as the New Zealanders *P. crassifolium*, *P. eugenioides* and *P. tenuifolium*, are also valued for their foliage, which is usually shiny and dark green with wavy edges, but may be silvery or bright yellow-green. Especially popular are the variegated cultivars which have leaves splashed with white or cream.

Some pittosporum species have decorative berries, such as *Pittosporum rhombifolium* (above). The cultivar *P. eugenioides* 'Variegatum' (right) makes an impressive hedge with its variegated leaves.

GROWING NOTES

Depending on the species, pittosporums may suit climates from tropical to cold. These plants are generally fast-growing, long-lived and very adaptable, although they are best in full sun and well-drained soil. Some species tolerate frost, wind and coastal conditions or can be grown in pots. Most pittosporums grow 5–10 metres (15–30 ft) in height, but can be clipped to keep them restrained.

PRUNUS LAUROCERASUS
CHERRY LAUREL

Most members of the great clan *Prunus* are known for their fruit or flowers, but the cherry laurel is grown for its leaves. Glossy, ovate and leathery dark green (bay-like, as its name suggests), its foliage forms a majestic canopy and, unlike the majority of its genus, the cherry laurel is evergreen. Its flowers differ, too. They are not the usual spring blossoms of *Prunus*, borne on bare branches, but produced on upright spikes instead. Small, white and scented, the flowers are followed by decorative cherry-like fruits. Cherry laurels grow into dense trees about 6 metres (18 ft) in height, but are most frequently seen clipped into hedges and screens. Cultivars include dwarf forms ideal for low hedging and containers.

GROWING NOTES
Cherry laurels are best in cool to cold, moist climates, and are long-lived in these conditions. They will also adapt to warmer gardens, but not the tropics. The plants grow in sun or shade, and tolerate exposed situations. They prefer rich, well-drained soil and regular watering during warm, dry seasons.

Cherry laurels make majestic hedges of uniform and glossy green leaves; they are also trouble-free and can be very long-lived.

SANTOLINA CHAMAECYPARISSUS
COTTON LAVENDER

Traditionally clipped in knot gardens and low hedges, cotton lavender also suits informal designs where it can be featured for its summer flowers as well as its leaves.

One of the best purveyors of silver in the garden, the cotton lavender has been cultivated for centuries, both as a herb and decoratively. It is a favourite of knot gardens, especially in contrasting edges or patterns, but also of neutral-coloured designs and modern 'all-white' schemes. Not related to lavender but part of the daisy family, cotton lavenders are evergreen and low-growing, to about 60 cm (2 ft) in height and width. The shrubs have naturally dense, compact habits with many branches of deeply serrated, aromatic leaves—creating their trademark mounds of fine silvery-grey foliage. Unclipped, the cotton lavender blooms in summer, with rounded yellow flowerheads adding to its appeal.

GROWING NOTES

Cotton lavender originates in the Mediterranean region; however, it suits most climates from warm to cool, except the tropics. The plants require full sun and well-drained soil. Once established, they tolerate dry spells. Even as clipped features, cotton lavenders are low-maintenance. An occasional light trim, such as after flowering, is all they need to keep them shapely.

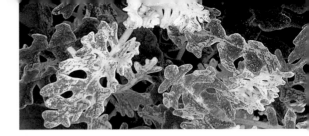

SENECIO CINERARIA

DUSTY MILLER

There's a lot of horticultural debate over the dusty miller's botanical name. Although experts agree that it is part of the daisy family, the plant is variously classified as *Cineraria* (which, appropriately, means ash-coloured), *Senecio* (that great genus of more than 1,200 species) or *Artemisia* (the wormwoods, see page 128). Fortunately, its common name is universal to gardeners, and dusty miller is easily distinguished by its deeply serrated, ghostly grey-green leaves. The foliage has an extraordinary felt-like texture that softly reflects light and gives it a shimmering white appearance. Dusty miller blends well in mixed borders, and is much favoured in garden designs of silver, white or grey.

Although dusty millers are mostly grown for their silvery leaves, their summer blooms will also provide bright contrasts of yellow-gold.

GROWING NOTES

Dusty millers originate in the Mediterranean region and are best in similar conditions; however, these plants will grow in most climates from warm to cool. They prefer full sun, open aspects and well-drained soil. Evergreen shrubs, dusty millers grow about 1 metre (3 ft) in height and twice as wide, and have naturally dense and rounded habits.

STROBILANTHES DYERIANUS
PERSIAN SHIELD

With its dazzling leaves of purple, pink and silver etched in green, the Persian shield is an evergreen shrub that brightens the garden year round. It's also often grown in pots, and indoors, bringing an exotic touch of the tropics into our homes. The leaves of the Persian shield aren't just colourful, they're large, up to 15 cm (6 inches) long, and the plant grows into a loose, rounded shrub, about 1 metre (3 ft) tall and usually wider, forming a dramatic foliage display. Although the plant does produce spikes of pale blue flowers, this only occurs in hot tropical climates and the blooms are not as exciting as its leaves.

The brightly coloured foliage of the Persian shield will bring warm, shady gardens to life; these shrubs also make dramatic indoor displays.

GROWING NOTES

All *Strobilanthes* prefer tropical or subtropical climates. They also suit warm gardens, but won't tolerate frost. In cooler areas, they can be grown indoors. The plants require dappled light or part shade, such as a few hours of morning sun; but in tropical areas, they will grow in full shade. The soil should be fairly rich with organic matter and well drained. Water generously in spring and summer.

flowering
trees

Trees are the most outstanding living features in any natural landscape, and also in our cities, parks and gardens. But when a tree flowers, it's a special occasion. All over the world, many of our cultural celebrations coincide with trees in bloom. In the garden, flowering trees are defining features. They highlight the seasons with their blooms, and will also inspire designs.

Trees in flower highlight the seasons and, over the years, or centuries, they become integral features of the garden. This page: A pathway lined with flowering Higan cherries. Previous pages: *Magnolia* x *soulangiana* cultivar.

This chapter features trees that are famous for their flowers. Some of these have outrageously colourful blooms, or hold spectacular tree-covering shows; others have flowers that are especially fragrant. Also throughout this book, you will find many other trees and shrubs that are prized for their foliage or fruit, as well as flowers. For gardeners, there are flowering trees to suit any style.

Flowering trees will define the character of a garden scene with their structure, growing habits and seasonal blooms. Left: Flowering cherry 'Sieboldii'. Right: Frangipani bloom. Following pages: Californian lilac and tamarisk as features.

The Australian wattles are the most popular *Acacia*; there are many hundreds of species and cultivars, with the majority flowering in winter or spring.

ACACIA SPECIES
ACACIA

There are more than a thousand naturally occurring types of *Acacia*, including the Australian wattles and the African thorn trees, making this an enormous genus of plants. Even among the wattles alone, there are hundreds of species. Both in their homeland and throughout the world, wattles are valued for their fast-growing evergreen habits, with a variety of leaf shapes, and fluffy golden-yellow flowers which are their hallmark. Some of the most popular wattles include the Cootamundra wattle (*Acacia baileyana*), with fine grey-green leaves; the golden wattle (*A. pycnantha*), the floral emblem of Australia; and the silver wattle or mimosa (*A. dealbata*), which has been cultivated in Europe for more than 200 years, and has also naturalised there, demonstrating its great adaptability.

GROWING NOTES
There are acacias for all climates except the extremely cold. Most of the commonly grown wattles are able to endure varying degrees of drought, frost and coastal conditions. The plants require full sun for best flowering, and must have well-drained soil. Water regularly to establish the trees. Acacias can be short-lived, especially the smaller species.

ALBIZIA JULIBRISSIN

SILK TREE

C losely related to the wattles, the silk tree is easily distinguished by its fluffy tassel-like flowers, which appear like puffs of colour all over the tree, but also by its peculiar habit of folding up its leaves at night. Originating from south-western Asia and Japan, silk trees are ornamental gems of the garden. They are fast-growing but not too unwieldy, and rarely grow more than 8 metres (24 ft) tall or wide. Their canopies are fluttery and airy, comprised of many narrow leaflets, and cast light shade. The silk tree's trademark flower tassel is actually created by a bunch of very fine stamens: in the species, these are cream with pink tips, but there are also colour-enhanced cultivars.

Silk trees flower in late spring and summer. These deciduous trees are trouble-free in the garden, and easy to incorporate into designs.

GROWING NOTES

Silk trees are very adaptable to frost-free climates from tropical to cool. They are best in full sun and open aspects. The trees will grow in any well-drained soil. However, they flower better if conditions aren't too rich, and because they are legumes, their roots will improve the nitrogen content of soils.

BAUHINIA SPECIES & CULTIVARS
BAUHINIA

The exquisite beauty of the bauhinias' blooms have earned them such common names as orchid trees, however, these plants actually belong to the same family as peas. So while their flowers are exotic, bauhinias can be surprisingly hardy. There are many species and cultivars of *Bauhinia*, but the most frequently grown are the trees. These include the butterfly tree, *Bauhinia purpurea*, which can grow to about 10 metres (30 ft) in height; as well as the smaller-growing, purple orchid tree, *B. variegata*, and its white-flowered form. Also popular is the hybrid, *B. x blakeana*, which only grows 2–3 metres (6-9 ft) tall; it is often called the Hong Kong orchid tree and has long racemes of fragrant red-purple blooms.

GROWING NOTES

Most of the commonly grown bauhinias are best in warm to tropical climates; they will also adapt to cooler regions and endure a light, rare frost. The plants prefer full sun and well-drained soil that is enriched with organic matter. Protect them from strong or cold wind. They must be watered regularly during hot weather.

Most bauhinias flower throughout spring and summer. The blooms are usually bright purple or cerise, but there are also forms with orange or white flowers.

CALLISTEMON SPECIES & CULTIVARS
BOTTLEBRUSH

The distinct flowerhead of the bottlebrush is actually a prolific stamen display, and the botanical name of the genus, *Callistemon*, literally means 'beautiful stamens'. For these, the bottlebrush is known, and cultivated, in gardens all over the world. Although there are only about 25 species in this all-Australian genus, the bottlebrushes grow wild in a range of habitats, and are remarkably adaptable—some tolerate light frost, pollution and drought; others grow in pots or heavy soil. Recently, a new wave of cultivars has become widely available (adding to an already extensive selection), and these bottlebrushes are even easier to grow. Also, where red once predominated, there are now many forms with flowerheads of pink, yellow or cream.

GROWING NOTES

There are bottlebrush species and cultivars to suit garden climates from cool to tropical. The plants are best in full sun and well-drained soil, but they are very adaptable to soil conditions. Bottlebrushes are evergreen and grow fairly quickly. To keep plants compact, trim flowers as soon as they finish; mature trees can be pruned hard to rejuvenate them.

Bottlebrushes are usually small trees or large shrubs, but there are also forms that are low-growing; their main flowering season is spring, but they can bloom again in autumn.

CAPE CHESTNUT

Native to South Africa, the cape chestnut is an evergreen with glossy, ovate leaves; grafted forms are fairly fast-growing and quick to produce clusters of pink flowers.

The popularity of the cape chestnut used to be somewhat hampered by its slowness to flower, with seedling trees taking at least a decade, or more, to reach maturity. These days, however, grafted trees are widely available and will flower within three or four years. It's worth any wait. Eventually, the cape chestnut can grow to 10–15 metres (30–45 ft) in height, with a broad-domed crown up to 8 metres (24 ft) wide—in full bloom, it's a sight to savour. The flowers are silvery-pink and borne in profuse panicles that frothily cover the tree in late spring and summer, and they are fragrant, too.

GROWING NOTES

Cape chestnuts are evergreens that grow best in warm to tropical climates. They will adapt to cooler gardens, where they may become deciduous, but will endure only the lightest of frosts. The trees prefer full sun, protection from strong wind, and well-drained soil that is enriched with organic matter. Water the plants regularly during spring and summer to promote good growth.

CEANOTHUS SPECIES & CULTIVARS
CALIFORNIAN
LILAC

There are many species of *Ceanothus*, a genus from western North America, but most of them originate in California. All have brilliant blue flowers, for which these plants are famed. However, their flower colours do vary—from powdery blue to deepest amethystine—and so can the plants' habits and forms. Californian lilacs may be low-growing, like the prostrate *Ceanothus impressus*, or become small trees, such as *C. thyrsiflorus*, which can reach 5–6 metres (15–18 ft) in height. Most are evergreen, but a few are deciduous. There are also many hybrids and cultivars, including a pink-flowered form and, of course, a wondrous range of blues.

GROWING NOTES

Californian lilacs suit cool to mild climates, but are best in regions with hot, dry summers and cold, wet winters. They dislike humidity, especially in summer, and appreciate good air circulation. The plants require full sun and well-drained soil. They are very susceptible to root rot in heavy clay or waterlogged conditions. Tip-prune after flowering to keep the plants compact and tidy; remove the lowest branches to encourage broad vase shapes.

There are many forms of Californian lilac, from groundcovers to large shrubs and small trees. Most types flower in spring, but some will also continue in summer.

CERCIS SILIQUASTRUM
JUDAS TREE

The Judas tree has appealing habits, and doesn't deserve its grim association with the betrayer of Christ, Judas Iscariot, who, according to legend, met his end under *Cercis siliquastrum*. Originating in the Mediterranean area, and a member of the pea family, this deciduous tree is an attractive vase-shape when young, and matures to about 5–8 metres (15–24 ft) in gardens, with a rounded or oval crown. It has unusual leaves, heart-shaped and partly folded, of pleasant blue-green. The flowers are cheerful and bright, appearing in small bunches and covering the bare branches from late winter to mid-spring, and these are followed by decorative pods. And, unlike its namesake, the Judas tree is reliable as well.

The flowers of the Judas tree are bright lilac-pink in the species but may be white in cultivars; the blooms appear before leaves form in spring.

GROWING NOTES

The Judas tree is easy to grow in climates from cool to subtropical; however, it is best with hot, dry summers and cool, wet winters. The plants prefer full sun, in an open position, and well-drained soil. Water the trees regularly to establish them, but also in spring or during very dry seasons.

CHIONANTHUS SPECIES
FRINGE TREE

The cloud-like effect of the fringe tree in full bloom is created by its narrow-petalled flowers, which cover its bare-branched canopy for a few weeks in spring. Ornamental gems, there are only two species of *Chionanthus* commonly cultivated: *Chionanthus retusus*, the Chinese fringe tree, with its superfine blooms, and *C. virginicus*, from the United States, which has pendulous sprays of larger flowers. Both deciduous, with bright yellow autumn foliage colour, the trees will grow 6–10 metres (18–30 ft) in height. Fairly slow to mature, but worth the wait, they are best planted where their naturally broad and rounded crowns can develop unrestricted, such as in spacious borders or woodland-style gardens.

Flowers with fine narrow petals give the fringe tree its common name. They cover the canopy in a creamy-white haze, and are lightly scented, too.

GROWING NOTES
The fringe trees prefer full sun in cool, moist climates. However, they will also grow in suitable microclimates in temperate regions, if shaded from hot afternoon sun. They prefer moist but well-drained soil, enriched with organic matter. Water regularly during dry periods in spring and summer. The trees need protection from strong wind, which spells disaster for the flowers.

CORNUS SPECIES & CULTIVARS
DOGWOOD

Unlike other blossom trees with their petals aflutter, the dogwood's flowering display has a rare quality. In most of the trees in the genus *Cornus*, the flowers are tiny and insignificant, and it is the floral bracts which put on the colourful show—from pristine white through the prettiest shades of pale pink to almost red.

Dogwoods have a natural affinity with cool, woodland-style gardens. They can also be planted as features of borders, or in groves.

Dogwoods originate in the cool forests of Europe, Asia and northern America, and have been cultivated for centuries—for practical purposes, such as fruit, wood and roots (which yield dye), as well as for bracts. Dogwoods are ornamental in all seasons. Most are deciduous, with richly toned autumn leaves and refined structures displayed in winter when the branches are bare. They also have decorative clusters of fruit, which follow the spring flowers, and ripen to crimson in summer.

Treasures of the woodland garden and romantic designs, there are many popular species of dogwoods, as well as cultivars. These include *Cornus florida*, which grows to about 6 metres (18 ft) in height, with a spreading canopy; the taller and more slender Pacific dogwood, *C. nuttallii*, with large white bracts; and *C. alba*, which is grown, not for flowers, but for its bright red bark in winter.

Most dogwoods, including *Cornus florida* (opposite) and *C. kousa* (above left), are deciduous and flower in spring, usually before their new leaves form.

GROWING NOTES

All the dogwoods are best in cool, moist climates. However, some also adapt to suitable microclimates in slightly warmer or colder gardens. The trees grow in full sun or dappled shade, depending on the type. They require protection from strong wind, rich, well-drained soil, and regular watering during spring and summer. If required, prune lightly to enhance the tree's shape. Coloured-stem cultivars should be cut back in late winter or very early spring to induce new growth.

CRATAEGUS SPECIES & CULTIVARS
HAWTHORN

The English hawthorn flowers profusely in spring; it has many cultivars, including some with double blooms.

The hawthorn may be best known as an essential spiny ingredient of the English-style hedgerow, but it's also a decorative garden tree. As well as fragrant blossoms in spring, hawthorns feature attractive lobed leaves, which are colourful in autumn, and most have bright red berries throughout autumn and winter, too. Of the 200 or so species of hawthorns, all deciduous, *Crataegus laevigata*, the English hawthorn (actually endemic throughout Europe), is the most commonly grown; popular, too, are its cultivars that have double flowers of white, pink and red. The tree naturally grows about 8 metres (24 ft) tall, but can be restrained to half that height in screens and hedges.

GROWING NOTES

Most hawthorns grow in warm to cold climates, but they are best in cooler areas. They require full sun, revel in open aspects, and tolerate extreme exposure to wind. The plants are quite adaptable to soil types, though deep and well-drained is preferred. Remove the lowest branches to encourage vase-like tree shapes, or prune after flowering if using plants in hedging—but wear protective clothing.

DELONIX REGIA
POINCIANA

From the treasure trove of plant and animal life that is Madagascar, gardeners have received many gifts—and among the greatest of these is the poinciana. First 'discovered' more than two centuries ago, and a genus of only one species, *Delonix regia* is now quite rare in the wild, but commonly cultivated in tropical climes. In height, the poinciana is moderate, usually no more than 8–10 metres (24–30 ft) tall, but its breadth is tremendous, with a canopy of near-horizontal branches that may spread 15–20 metres (45–60 ft) wide. In summer, when the awesome crown is covered in swathes of scarlet flowers, it's easy to see why the poinciana is regarded as one of the world's most spectacular trees.

GROWING NOTES

Poincianas are best in tropical climates, but they also adapt to subtropical gardens in suitably warm situations. In the tropics, these trees are evergreen; elsewhere, they are semi-deciduous. The plants prefer full sun, protection from strong wind, and well-drained soil, with plenty of water in summer.

Few trees can rival the poinciana's dazzling flower display, which covers its impressive canopy for weeks in summer.

The gordonia's flowering display lasts for many months on the tree throughout the cooler seasons, but the blooms are still ornamental after they fall to the ground.

GORDONIA AXILLARIS
GORDONIA

The gordonia is a garden favourite with many great attributes. Its autumn and winter flowers are fragrant and large, each up to 7 cm (5 inches) in diameter, and have soft, diaphanous-white, frilled petals and outstanding clusters of sunny-yellow stamens. The tree is evergreen, growing to a tractable 5–8 metres (15–24 ft) in height, with a broad canopy of glossy, leathery leaves. During cold winters, some of the foliage may turn startling red and a few leaves may fall. Related to camellias and originating from southern China and Vietnam, gordonias are very versatile—they suit streetscapes, woodland-style shrubberies and small gardens, and will also grow in pots.

GROWING NOTES

Gordonias thrive in temperate to tropical climates, but will also tolerate light frost. They prefer dappled shade or morning sun only. The soil should be well drained, enriched with organic matter, and acidic (gordonias don't like lime). Water regularly to establish the trees, and during dry warm seasons. Although naturally graceful, gordonias may also be pruned to shape; remove the lowest branches to create a vase-like habit.

GREVILLEA SPECIES & CULTIVARS
GREVILLEA

The great range of grevilleas includes new hybrids and cultivars for gardens, such as the shrub-like forms 'Honey Gem' (above left) and 'Moonlight' (above right).

The grevillea is one of Australia's unique flowering trees, with more than 250 species found across the country. All the grevilleas share a distinctive brush-style flower—though these may be spidery, spike-like or one-sided—but the plants can vary greatly in habit from tall trees to groundcovers. The largest grevillea, and probably the most widely grown until recently, is *Grevillea robusta*, the silky oak: it can reach more than 35 metres (100 ft) in height, but is also commonly grown in pots and indoors. In the past few years, the hybrid grevilleas and cultivars have become deservedly popular. These are mostly fast-growing shrubs, evergreen and adaptable, with an amazing range of flowers.

GROWING NOTES
Of the many grevillea species and cultivars, there are plants to suit all climates from tropical to cold. In general, they prefer full sun and require very well drained soil. Once established, the plants are tolerant of drought. Tip-prune regularly after flowering to keep the trees compact and productive.

HAMAMELIS SPECIES & CULTIVARS
WITCH HAZEL

The witch hazels are a distinctive group, from eastern Asia and North America, with only a handful of species, distinguished by broadly ovate leaves and yellow flowers with four narrow petals, often twisted. They include the Virginian witch hazel, *Hamamelis virginiana*, of significant medicinal and astringent fame, and the ornamental species, such as the Japanese witch hazel, *H. japonica*, and the Chinese witch hazel, *H. mollis*, both of which have fragrant, late winter flowers. All witch hazels are deciduous, and grow 2–10 metres (6–30 ft) in height, depending on the type. As well as for flowers, these plants are prized for autumn foliage colour, their uncommonly rounded leaves turning bright yellow-gold.

Witch hazels provide welcome, late winter flowers. *Hamamelis mollis* (above and right), with fragrant blooms, is one of the most ornamental forms for gardens.

GROWING NOTES

Witch hazels are best in cool to cold, moist climates. Both the plants and their flowers will survive frost. They grow in full sun or part shade, and require protection from hot wind. The soil should be well drained, rich and preferably slightly acidic. The trees are slow-growing but long-lived. Flowering branches may be cut for indoor decoration.

ILLICIUM ANISATUM
ANISE TREE

Although cultivated commercially for its fruit, star-anise (which is used as a spice) and for its bark (which is made into incense), the anise tree is featured and favoured in gardens because of its flowers. These are starry, with many petals of pale yellow, and potently fragrant. Originating from China and from Japan, where it has sacred Buddhist associations, *Illicium anisatum* is an evergreen with thick, glossy, ovate leaves and grows slowly to about 8 metres (24 ft) in height. Another popular species is the purple anise, *I. floridanum*, from southern North America, which has shrub-like habits and purple–red flowers in early summer.

GROWING NOTES

The anise tree is best in temperate to tropical climates, but will also grow in cooler areas. The plants prefer part shade and well-drained soil that is enriched with organic matter. They need protection from strong wind, and a sheltered position will concentrate the fragrance of the flowers. Water regularly to establish, and also in spring and summer. If required, the plants can be lightly pruned to shape after flowering.

The aromatic blooms of the anise tree appear in spring. These evergreen trees are slow-growing but will flower when young.

JACARANDA MIMOSIFOLIA
JACARANDA

Jacarandas flower in spring or summer, depending on the climate; there is also a white-flowered cultivar.

Wherever they are grown, the flowering of jacarandas is a special occasion in the gardening year. Originating in Brazil, *Jacaranda mimosifolia* has been widely embraced: all over the world, many towns and cities celebrate the 'jacaranda season', when the trees that line their streets and feature in parks and gardens come into bloom. But even out-of-flower, the jacaranda is elegant, 10–15 metres (30–45 ft) in height and almost as wide, with a canopy that casts generous but light shade. Deciduous, the foliage turns a pleasant yellow then falls in late winter and spring. For a few weeks, the branches may be bared, revealing the tree's stately structure, before the famous flowers cover it in a purple haze.

GROWING NOTES
Jacarandas are best in temperate to tropical climates. They will endure the lightest of frosts, but grow slowly in these cooler conditions. The trees adapt to a range of soils, but require full sun and protection from strong wind. Long-lived and fast-growing, they may take several years to flower; grafted trees are quicker to bloom.

LABURNUM SPECIES & CULTIVARS
LABURNUM

There are only two species in this genus, *Laburnum*, of deciduous trees, both originating in northern Europe. The most significant of these, *Laburnum anagyroides*, is known for its pendulous sprays of yellow flowers which drip from the tree in spring and early summer. It has a lax habit, growing to about 7 metres (21 ft) in height, with a cascading canopy of fine leaves that are each comprised of three ovate leaflets; while the variety 'Pendula' has a more exaggerated weeping form. However, the most frequently grown laburnum is a hybrid of the two species, L. x *watereri*, named after the nursery where it was raised in the 1800s, and also commonly called the golden chain tree for its spectacular flowering racemes.

GROWING NOTES
Laburnums prefer cool to temperate climates, with cold winters. The plants require full sun, though they aren't particular about soil. Laburnums are long-lived and, with pliant stems, are very easy to train (for example, over arches and pergolas). Gardeners should be aware that all parts of laburnum plants are poisonous.

Laburnums are traditionally and romantically used to cover garden arbours and walls, but they also make graceful feature trees.

LAGERSTROEMIA INDICA
CREPE MYRTLE

When most other deciduous flowering trees are slowing down in late summer and autumn, the crepe myrtle bursts into bloom. The tree becomes covered in profuse trusses of ruffled blossoms—in shocking pinks, red, mauve or white—that retain their colour for weeks, even as they fall to the ground like confetti. After the flowers, its small and rounded leaves become the main attraction as they change from green to bright yellow, with highlights of orange and crimson. The tree's branches, bared in winter, are a feature, too, with mottled bark and a smooth satiny texture.

The crepe myrtle is an asset to the garden in all seasons, but is also very versatile: it's ideal for mixed borders or avenues, and in small gardens and containers, too.

GROWING NOTES

Lagerstroemia indica suits frost-free gardens, and thrives in warm to tropical climates. The plants are best in full sun, but also grow in light shade. They aren't fussy about soil, though well-drained is preferred. Water regularly to establish, after which the trees will tolerate dry periods. Many cultivars are available, varying in height at 2–10 metres (6–30 ft), including the Indian Summer range, which has all the flower colours as well as improved garden performance.

Magnolia x *soulangiana* remains the most popular of the magnolia hybrids; these have goblet-shaped flowers in a range of colours, including ivory, white and pink to purple and claret red.

MAGNOLIA SPECIES & CULTIVARS
MAGNOLIA

In the world of flowering trees, the magnolia is an aristocrat, belonging to one of the oldest plant families. Most species originate in the woodlands of Asia, and although relatively recent to western horticulture, having only been grown for a few centuries, these magnolias have been cultivated in China and Japan for thousands of years.

The most common magnolias in gardens are the deciduous types that flower, before the leaves appear, in late winter, spring or early summer. These include the many varieties of *Magnolia* x *soulangiana*, an influential hybrid which made its debut in France in the 1820s; *M. liliiflora* and its cultivars, with typically tulip-shaped flowers that are dark pink on the outside and paler inside; and the star magnolia, *M. stellata*, from Japan, which only grows 2–3 metres (6–9 ft) in height and has lax-petalled flowers of soft pastel pink tones.

Magnolia species favoured in gardens include the evergreen *Magnolia grandiflora* (right), and the star magnolia (below and opposite) from Japan.

From the other side of the world, M. *grandiflora* is the best-known of the evergreens. Native to North America, it matures at about 20 metres (60 ft) tall, with a classic, broad-dome shape that casts deep shade. It flowers from late spring to summer and early autumn, with decadently large, waxy-white blooms that have an intoxicatingly sweet fragrance.

GROWING NOTES

The deciduous magnolias prefer climates with cool to cold winters, but there are several species and hybrids that adapt well to warmer conditions. The evergreen, M. *grandiflora*, is best in warm to tropical climates. Most magnolias prefer full sun, although some will grow in part shade. The plants require well-drained, slightly acidic soil that is rich in organic matter. Many magnolias in gardens are grafted because the genus is notoriously slow to flower.

MALUS SPECIES & CULTIVARS
CRABAPPLE

Before there was the apple, there was the crabapple, growing wild in Europe and Asia. But a few thousand years ago, and influenced of course by humankind, the genus *Malus* went separate ways. The apple became domesticated (see pages 446–9) and eventually a main player in the global fruit-tree scene. The crabapple took the ornamental path and, even though it is still sometimes grown for fruit, it became known for blossoms instead—and is now one of the garden's favourite flowering trees.

Crabapples have been cultivated for centuries, especially in Japan, the epicentre of ornamental blossom trees. Many of the species and cultivars were raised in ancient Japanese gardens, and perfected into the forms we know today. These include *Malus floribunda*, often called the Japanese crabapple, with its red-budded, pale pink blooms; and *M. tschonoskii*, which has a

Most crabapples will flower in spring, usually before their foliage is formed. The hybrid 'Eleyi' (left) and the Japanese crabapple (above) are both very adaptable forms.

As well as spring flowers, crabapples, such as the hybrid *Malus* x 'Gorgeous' (left), have great garden assets including graceful habits, colourful autumn foliage, and fruit.

narrower habit than most forms, and spotted yellow-green fruit. However, one of the most popular crabapples is from northern America, *M. ioensis*, known as the Iowa crab, along with its double-flowered cultivar 'Plena'. Many hybrids have also been raised, including the aptly named *M.* x 'Gorgeous', from New Zealand, which has large fruits and blossoms.

GROWING NOTES

All the crabapples are deciduous trees, with lovely autumn leaf colours. They have graceful garden habits, usually growing 6–8 metres (18–24 ft) in height, with broad rounded crowns. Most prefer cool, moist climates, but some are very adaptable to warmer regions, such as *M. floribunda* and the well-known hybrid *M.* x *purpurea* 'Eleyi'. Crabapples are best in full sun, with protection from strong wind. They prefer well-drained soil, enriched with organic matter. Water regularly during spring and summer, especially in warm climates.

MICHELIA SPECIES
MICHELIA

MICHELIA

Michelias are renowned for their floral scent. The port wine magnolia (below) flowers in spring; *Michelia doltsopa* (right) has creamy-coloured, late winter blooms.

Although michelias are related to the magnolias, as can be seen from their exquisitely shaped blooms, their flowers are very small compared to their cousins' and inconspicuously huddled within dense canopies of glossy leaves. Instead, the michelia's floral energies are packed into creating memorable fragrances in the garden. Of the 30 or so species of these evergreen trees and shrubs from Asia, the best known is *Michelia figo*, the port wine magnolia, which grows to 5 metres (15 ft), but can also be used as a screen or informal hedge. Also desirable is *M. doltsopa*, a handsome tree about 10 metres (30 ft) in height, and *M. champaca*, which is taller-growing and valued in perfumery for the essential oils of its flowers.

GROWING NOTES

Michelias are suitable for frost-free climates, preferably warm to tropical. They require full sun and protection from strong wind. The soil should be well drained and enriched with organic matter. Water generously in spring and summer, especially if seasons are dry. If required, prune lightly after flowering to keep plants compact.

OSMANTHUS SPECIES & CULTIVARS
OSMANTHUS

The osmanthus may not have the most flamboyant of blooms, but it has one of the best perfumes—and its botanical name literally means 'fragrant flower'. A genus of evergreen trees and shrubs, *Osmanthus* originates in Asia and northern America, and all have clusters of pale and tiny flowers with remarkably powerful scents. *Osmanthus fragrans* is one of the more commonly grown, and its flowers are used in China to flavour tea (some say the floral undertones are orangey; others say ripe peach). Also popular is the autumn-flowering *O. heterophyllus*, with holly-shaped leaves, and its variegated cultivar; and the hybrid, *O.* x *fortunei*, which caught the eye (and nose) of plant hunter Robert Fortune in Japan in the late 1800s, and has been prized in gardens ever since.

GROWING NOTES

Osmanthus are suitable for climates from warm to cool. They prefer full sun and well-drained soil. Most forms grow into large shrubs or small trees, 1.5–3 metres (5–9 ft) in height, with broad canopies of glossy leaves. Their naturally compact habits rarely need pruning.

Commonly called the sweet olive, *Osmanthus fragrans* (opposite and above) is redolent with spring flowers.

PAULOWNIA SPECIES
PAULOWNIA

The paulownia's flowers unfurl over several weeks in spring. The trees will flower when young, but they are also fast-growing and trouble-free.

This small group of deciduous trees, with only six species endemic to China and eastern Asia, is closely related to foxgloves, as can be seen from their spires of hooded flowers. Fragrant, soft pale purple, sometimes with white throats, the paulownia's blooms are borne on upright racemes in early spring, usually on top of the bare branches before the foliage forms—a splendid sight on a full-grown tree of 15 metres (45 ft) in height, with a conical canopy 10 metres (30 ft) wide. Paulownias also have handsome leaves: heart-shaped, large, up to 30 cm (1 ft) in size, and downy, casting generous pools of dappled shade.

GROWING NOTES
Paulownias will grow in climates from warm to cool; however, late frosts in spring will damage the flower buds and ruin their moment of glory. The trees are best in full sun, with shelter from strong wind. They prefer deep, rich, well-drained soil, but aren't particularly fussy. Generous watering in spring and summer encourages fast and strong growth of the trees.

PLUMERIA RUBRA
FRANGIPANI

Many gardeners agree that the frangipani is a flower of paradise. Charles Plumier, the French plant hunter, must have thought so when he came across it in the late 1600s while exploring the Caribbean and Central America. In Buddhism and other Eastern religions, the frangipani is a symbol of eternity (for it can 'resurrect' from whole branches), and the trees are often planted in sacred places. In gardens, it is favoured in streetscapes, parks, groves and pots. Eventually growing to 6–8 metres (18–24 ft) in height and width, with thick branches and leathery leaves, frangipanis will flower as very young plants—and just a single tree will bring a slice of heaven to the garden.

Frangipanis are deciduous, but in tropical climates they flower year round. The blooms may be red, pink or white with yellow, or a combination of all these colours.

GROWING NOTES
Although best in temperate to tropical climates, frangipanis also grow in cooler conditions if protected from frost. They prefer full sun and rich, well-drained soil. While the trees can be quite tolerant of drought, they will lose their precious flowers and leaves. Be aware of the sap, which can irritate the skin and is poisonous.

PRUNUS SPECIES & CULTIVARS
FLOWERING PRUNUS

Although they are the definitive blossom trees of spring, prunus may flower in midwinter or early summer instead. The flowering cherries (above) and plums (opposite) are very popular forms.

It's no mystery why the flowering forms of the genus *Prunus* are so widely planted. With a tantalising palette of flower colours, and such attractive forms, these trees are addictive. Many gardeners find that one leads to a collection—and before long, a grove is born.

The flowering cherry, *Prunus serrulata*, has been cultivated in Japan since about the sixth century. It was the ancient Japanese who turned blossoms into an art form, and also started the trend of festivities under these trees when they first held blossom-viewing parties many centuries ago. Today, most flowering cherries in cultivation descend from *P. serrulata*; but also significant is the Higan cherry, *P. subhirtella*, and the Yoshino, *P.* x *yedoensis*.

Peaches, *P. persica* and cultivars, have been grown in their native China for thousands of years. There are many flowering types, and most have fragrant, double blooms, in white,

The diverse range of ornamental prunus includes the flowering peach (opposite), which suits warm gardens; the apricot (left) with its early blooms; and the Taiwan cherry (below).

various shades of pink or red. One amazing cultivar, 'Versicolour', has white, pink and red flowers on a single tree.

Also popular are flowering plums, such as *P. cerasifera*, and its cultivar 'Nigra', with deep purple foliage, and the hybrid *P.* x *blireana*. Aficionados also favour the Taiwan cherry, *P. campanulata*, with its bell-shaped, red blooms, and the ornamental apricot, *P. mume*, which, around midwinter, is the first of these prunus to flower.

GROWING NOTES

Flowering prunus are deciduous and will suit climates from cold to subtropical. Generally, the flowering cherries prefer cooler gardens, while the flowering peaches will only tolerate light frost. They all require full sun, shelter from strong wind, and rich, well-drained soil. The trees can range in height, growing 4–12 metres (12–36 ft) tall, and also in habit, from columnar or vase-shaped to weeping.

SPATHODEA CAMPANULATA
AFRICAN TULIP TREE

The African tulip tree really knows how to put on a flamboyant flower show. In late spring and summer, sometimes for months, its handsome crown plays host to trusses of flared, goblet-shaped flowers that are silky cinnabar with frilled edges of gold. This attention-grabbing display is enhanced by the tree's impressive height, up to 20 metres (60 ft) tall in its native tropical Africa, but less in cultivation, and its broad canopy of glossy compound leaves, that offers a good view of the blooms. Resilient, too, the African tulip tree is often planted in streetscapes in suitably warm climates, and is a trouble-free feature of tropical-style gardens.

GROWING NOTES
African tulip trees are best in tropical and subtropical regions; however, they may also be grown in sheltered, frost-free microclimates of warm gardens. They require full sun and protection from strong gales, which can topple them. The soil should be deep, enriched and well drained, and the trees need generous watering in spring and summer. In the right conditions, these are fairly fast-growing trees that don't suffer from pests or diseases.

The African tulip tree is also known as flame of the forest. It blooms for months, with flowers shimmering orange-red and edged in gold.

SYRINGA SPECIES & CULTIVARS
LILAC

The lilac tree is renowned for its purple-blue flowers, and is synonymous with the colour, but, over its long cultivation history, the genus *Syringa* has developed many varieties—and now the flowers of lilacs may be white, pink, red, or even pale yellow. The Persian lilac, *Syringa* x *persica*, was the favourite of ancient times but this has been overshadowed by the common lilac, *S. vulgaris*, and its hybrids and cultivars. Deciduous and spring-flowering like all lilacs, these modern types are usually multi-stemmed, and can grow into large shrubs or small trees, 3–7 metres (9–21 ft) in height. Among the numerous named forms there is a range of colours, but also double flowers, and some with supersized trusses of blooms.

Lilacs are famous for their fragrant blooms of unique purple-blue, but there are also many cultivars of various flower colours.

GROWING NOTES
Lilacs prefer cool to cold, moist climates, although a few cultivars will adapt to temperate gardens. They require full sun, with shelter from strong wind, and very rich, well-drained soil that is preferably slightly alkaline. Water regularly throughout the warm seasons. Rejuvenate mature trees by removing old, unproductive stems at ground level.

TAMARIX SPECIES
TAMARISK

Depending on the species, tamarisks may flower in spring or summer; the blooms, produced on long spikes, will cover the tree.

The tamarisks are much tougher than they appear, with their fine or feathery leaves and plumes of flowers in fluffy, colourful clouds. In fact, tamarisks will take some of the harshest garden conditions, including saline soils, sea spray, strong winds, and even drought once established. They are fast-growing, too, but not formidable. Most of the commonly grown types, such as the Caspian tamarisk, *Tamarix ramosissima*, and its cultivars, will rarely exceed 4–6 metres (12–18 ft) in height; these trees have open canopies that allow them to mingle with other plants in a variety of garden styles and designs.

GROWING NOTES

Most tamarisks are deciduous, although *T. aphylla*, the athel tree, is an evergreen. Tamarisks generally grow well in a range of climates, from subtropical and warm to cool. They are best in full sun and open aspects. The soil must be well drained and preferably sandy or gravelly. Newly planted trees should be watered regularly to get them established. If required, prune after flowering to keep the foliage dense.

TIBOUCHINA SPECIES & CULTIVARS
LASIANDRA

The vividly coloured, large and silken flowers of the lasiandra are the trademarks of this tree—a fabulous sight when in full, voluptuous bloom. Most famously, the lasiandra's flowers are jewel purple, but, depending on the variety, they can be equally stunning in white or rose-pink. Originating in South America, and mostly from Brazil, *Tibouchina* includes more than 300 species of evergreen shrubs and small trees: such as *Tibouchina granulosa*, which grows to 10 metres (30 ft) in height, and *T. urvilleana*, with flowers that are 12 cm (5 inches) in size. There are also many cultivars of lasiandras, including low-growing forms, less than 1 metre (3 ft) tall, that are ideal for flamboyant containers and borders.

GROWING NOTES
Lasiandras are best in frost-free, warm to tropical climates. The plants require full sun all day, and protection from strong or cold winds. The soil should be well drained and enriched with aged organic matter. Water regularly during warm seasons to ensure the best display of blooms. Tip-prune in early spring to keep growth compact, but not during cold weather.

The lasiandra, also known as the glory bush, will flower for months, from late summer throughout autumn, and sometimes into winter as well.

CAMELLIA SPECIES & CULTIVARS

camellia

Camellias have set a benchmark in ornamental trees. They excel in the desirable garden qualities: classic good looks; glossy evergreen leaves; adaptability to various climates; versatility in designs; and longevity, often outlasting the gardener in the garden. Then there's the range of flowers—perfected over centuries and each like a living work of art.

Although the camellia has been cultivated for thousands of years in China and Japan, most of its ornamental forms have only been known to European horticulture for a few centuries, after tea—*Camellia sinensis*—unlocked the doors of trade. Then, as now, few *Camellia* species are grown in gardens, but these have been enormously prolific in producing hybrids and cultivars. Today, there are so many camellias for gardeners to choose from that the International Camellia Register works hard to keep up, and most camellias are now described by flower type—single, semi-double, formal double, peony-form or informal double, and anemone-form—creating a common language for camellia enthusiasts worldwide.

Camellia japonica was the first of the ornamental species to be mass-cultivated, and, for many gardeners, it remains the archetypal camellia. The japonicas, as these cultivars are casually known, are the classic camellia trees, growing slowly but steadily with dense habits to 6–10 metres (18–30 ft) tall. They have set the standard for camellia flower colours, from white to crimson and every conceivable shade of pink in between, as well as streaks, vignettes and two-tones.

Modern garden camellias are defined by their flower forms, and also by their ancestry: the japonicas (opposite) are the most prolific group of hybrids and cultivars, descending from the species *Camellia japonica*.

Camellias inspire great garden designs. As well as featuring in formal borders and woodland styles, some camellias can be grown in containers, trained as espaliers or standards, or create outstanding hedges, like these sasanquas.

The sasanqua, *Camellia sasanqua*, is much valued for its garden vigour, a trait that has been passed on to its many cultivars and hybrids. They have the full range of flower forms and colours, and, although their blooms are more fragile than other camellias, sasanquas are tough. The plants vary greatly in habit, from low-growing shrubs to small trees, and adapt to a wide range of garden conditions and climates.

Also significant is the species *Camellia reticulata*, which has long been ornamentally cultivated in China but was only introduced to Europeans in the 1820s, via the Dutch East India Company. Valued because its flowers are larger and more flamboyant than other camellias, the species is, however, rather sparse in habit and so its cultivars and hybrids are often preferred. These combine attractive and vigorous growth with *C. reticulata*'s naturally spectacular blooms.

Most camellias in gardens are hybrids combining these three main species. However, other species are starting to make a presence on the camellia scene. *Camellia saluenensis*, a small shrub with flowers 5–7 cm (2–3 inches) in size, was only 'discovered' less than a century ago and has produced the floriferous and hardy hybrid *C.* x *williamsii*, one of the most popular camellia types today. Also increasingly significant is *C. lutchuensis*, a species with small, single blooms that has contributed fragrance to the modern camellia's charms.

From just a few camellia species, there are thousands of cultivars. They have flowers in every shade of red and pink to white, and an array of forms, from doubles teeming with petals to singles of simple beauty.

GROWING NOTES

Camellias are very adaptable as a group and grow in climates from cold to subtropical. They do tolerate light frost, but it will ruin their flowers. The plants aren't suitable for tropical conditions or hot arid areas. Most camellias are best in dappled shade or filtered sunlight. However, some, like the sasanquas and reticulatas, will grow in full sun. A general rule is that cultivars with dark-coloured blooms will take stronger light, but those with pale pink or white flowers require more shade.

The plants' main requirement in cultivation is slightly acidic soil which is well drained and enriched with organic matter. Camellias are especially susceptible to root rot in heavy or waterlogged soils; however, they do require even moisture, with regular watering in spring and summer. Many camellia types, such as the japonicas, sasanquas and small-flowered hybrids, are ideal for growing in pots, and so even without a great deal of space, gardeners can form quite a collection.

There are many good camellias widely available, but for something special, it's worthwhile contacting a specialist grower or nursery who can advise you on the forms available and their growing needs. There are also societies worldwide which are dedicated to the camellia.

The camellias' flowering season is usually from early autumn until late spring, depending on the cultivar and the garden's climate.

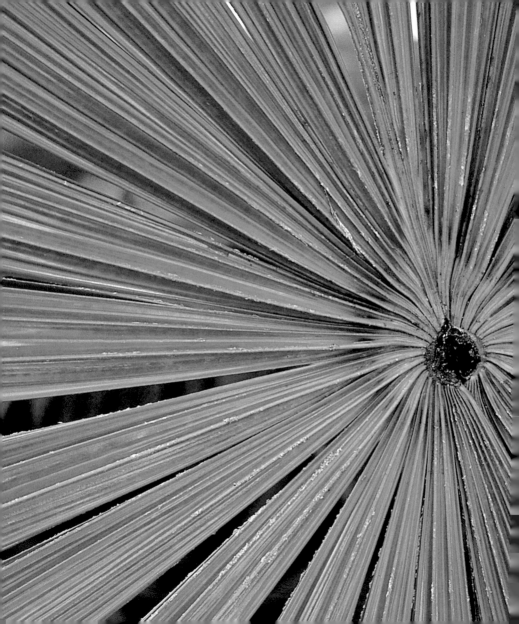

evergreen
trees

Trees are the foundations of garden designs, and evergreen trees, in particular, are influential features. All year round, these trees provide structure, shade and shelter, as well as seasonal fruit and flower. In gardens, they create enduring themes, from formal designs and streetscapes to wild woodlands or tropical styles, and even a single evergreen can create an evocative scene.

Evergreen trees have a presence in the garden in all seasons, throughout the years, and sometimes centuries. This page: A design of trees including evergreen hedges and conifers. Previous pages: The fan palm, *Licuala grandis*.

This chapter includes a range of evergreen trees, from favoured ornamentals, such as conifers and palms, to uncommon jewels, like the dragon's blood tree. Many others are also valued in gardens for flowers or fruit, and some of these can be found elsewhere in this book. Among the myriad evergreens available, there are trees for every gardening climate and purpose.

There are evergreen trees for all kinds of garden styles, from parks and avenues to topiaries and indoor displays. This page: False cypresses, *Chamaecyparis* species. Following pages: A garden with conifers as feature plants.

Given the space it requires, the evergreen alder forms a broad and graceful canopy that casts plenty of shade; in spring, it has yellow catkins on the tips of the branches.

ALNUS ACUMINATA
EVERGREEN ALDER

Most of the alders are deciduous trees, familiar in Europe and the northern hemisphere, but the evergreen alder is one that retains its foliage all year round. Native to the mountains of Central and South America, *Alnus acuminata* (syn. *A. jorullensis*) can grow to 10–15 metres (30–45 ft) in height, with a spread of 8 metres (24 ft). Evergreen alders are much favoured in large gardens and modern landscaping because the trees grow quickly and have graceful, generous canopies of weeping leaves. They also have a hidden asset: the roots of these trees can fix nitrogen in the soil, and hence improve the fertility of soil where they grow.

GROWING NOTES

Evergreen alders are best in warm climates. They grow in sheltered parts of cooler gardens, but will only tolerate the lightest frost. The trees prefer deep soil and open aspects; and require plenty of water, especially in warmer seasons. Importantly, they have voracious root systems and should not be planted close to houses and structures where their greedy roots may cause harm.

BUTIA CAPITATA
WINE PALM

The wine palm is one of the most versatile of its kind. Although native only to South America, it adapts to a wide range of climates, from coastal gardens to arid inland regions, and it even tolerates light frost. Wine palms are long-lived, but will also grow for years in pots. They are great feature palms, with silvery-green arching fronds forming a broad feathery crown. Eventually, these palms will form a stout trunk and will reach 5–6 metres (15–18 ft) in height; however, they are also attractive when young. Also known as the jelly palm, *Butia capitata* has male and female flowers on the same tree, and produces fruits which, though edible, ripen from yellow to red and add to its decorative qualities.

Wine palms are outstanding with their distinctive crowns of arching fronds. These palms are also very adaptable to a range of garden conditions.

GROWING NOTES
Wine palms grow in all but the coldest garden climates. They are best in full sun and open aspects. The soil should be well drained, though the plants aren't particular about type and will even grow in alkaline soils. Water regularly to establish, after which these palms are fairly drought resistant.

Cedars, like the deodar (above and right), are best in large gardens; however, some cultivars are slightly smaller than the species, such as *Cedrus atlantica* 'Glauca' (top).

CEDRUS SPECIES & CULTIVARS
CEDAR

Although there are only four species of *Cedrus*, the cedars are highly influential members of the conifer family. Three of them take their places among the famous trees of the world—the cedar of Lebanon (*Cedrus libani*), that venerable giant of spreading branches and foliage tiers; the atlas cedar (*C. atlantica*), with its distinct ascending branches and spiralled leaves; and the deodar (*C. deodara*), from the western Himalayas, with its layered, cascading canopy. These cedars are rarely found outside of parks and large gardens, limited by their impressive size; however, there are also some slightly smaller cultivars. These include the bluish-leaved form of the atlas cedar, *C. atlantica* 'Glauca', and *C. deodara* 'Aurea', a cultivar of the deodar with yellow-tipped foliage.

GROWING NOTES
The more common cedars are quite adaptable to climates from warm to cool. In general, the plants will not tolerate extreme hot, tropical or cold conditions, and they prefer moist environments. Most cedars in cultivation will reach heights of 20–30 metres (60–90 ft). They are best in deep soil and open aspects where they can grow unrestricted.

CHAMAECYPARIS SPECIES & CULTIVARS
FALSE CYPRESS

False cypresses are distinguished by their fanned sprays of flat leaves; there are many cultivars to suit a great range of garden climates and designs.

From just a handful of species and with a relatively short cultivation history, the false cypress has become one of the best-known conifers in gardens throughout the world. There are hundreds of cultivars of the false cypress, mostly deriving from the north American species, *Chamaecyparis lawsoniana*, but also from the Hinoki cypress, *C. obtusa*, and the Sawara cypress, *C. pisifera*, from Japan. The false cypresses are available in a remarkable range of sizes and habits, from columnar to conical, as well as foliage colours. However, they are also very adaptable to garden climates and styles, and may be featured as screens, along avenues and in formal designs, mixed borders and also pots.

GROWING NOTES

Within the great range of false cypress cultivars, there are trees suitable for climates from cold to subtropical; they are, in general, the most reliable of conifers for warmer gardens where many others fail. The plants are best in full sun (especially the coloured-leaf varieties), and deep, rich, well-drained soil. Some types, once established, are quite resistant to drought.

CHAMAEDOREA SPECIES
PARLOUR &
BAMBOO PALMS

This genus of predominantly rainforest-dwelling plants, *Chamaedorea*, is the most commonly grown of palms in gardening. Two species dominate and are frequently cultivated in frost-free gardens and as indoor plants. The parlour palm, *Chamaedorea elegans*, has a solitary trunk and feathered fronds and grows to 2–3 metres (6–9 ft). Also popular is the bamboo palm, *C. seifrizii*, with slender canes in clusters, up to 2 metres (6 ft) in height, and feathery fronds along the upper parts of the stems. Both species also produce colourful inflorescences, even when grown indoors: these are yellow in the parlour palm, and bright orange-red in the bamboo palm.

GROWING NOTES
These palms thrive in most frost-free gardens, where they require shade or dappled sunlight. In cool climates, they are easily grown indoors. Both bamboo and parlour palms are known for their longevity, but they will also happily spend their lives in containers. They prefer well-drained soil and regular watering in dry seasons to promote growth.

Among the most popular of all palms, especially for indoor gardens, are the bamboo palm (left) and the parlour palm (below).

CHRYSALIDOCARPUS LUTESCENS
GOLDEN CANE PALM

This palm belongs to a very small genus of only three species from Madagascar, but, with its clusters of smooth straight stems, banded and gold, it is widely admired and grown. The golden cane palm is an ornamental favourite of warm and tropical gardens, but it is also very popular as a potted feature—in courtyards, on balconies and indoors. It has shiny feathery fronds with a graceful arching habit, and forms a dense and dramatic clump with many canes of varying ages and sizes. In ideal conditions, the palm can grow to 10 metres (30 ft) in height but it is usually much smaller in gardens.

GROWING NOTES

Golden cane palms will grow in most frost-free gardens, although they thrive best in warm and tropical conditions. They prefer full sun or part shade, but the stems only become golden in strong light. The soil should be well drained and enriched with aged organic matter. Protect from strong winds, and water regularly throughout the warmer seasons.

The banded stems of the golden cane palm develop as the plants age; they are gold when grown in the sun, but verdigris green in the shade.

CITHAREXYLUM SPINOSUM
FIDDLEWOOD

In cooler gardens, the fiddlewood's leaves will colour in late winter and spring before they are cast by the tree; fresh foliage immediately follows.

The fiddlewood is a tree of many talents. As its common name suggests, the tree's timber is used to make musical instruments; initially in the West Indies, where it originates, but now throughout the world. The fiddlewood is also fast-growing, making it a favourite of landscapers, but it doesn't grow too tall, about 10–12 metres (30–36 ft) in height, nor too wide. Usually evergreen in tropical climates, the tree forms a dense canopy of shiny, ovate leaves; in cooler gardens, it is semi-deciduous, with most of the foliage colouring to soft apricot or orange before it falls in spring. To top off its features, the fiddlewood produces sprays of creamy-white flowers from midsummer to early winter, depending on the climate, and these are strongly, sweetly fragrant as well.

GROWING NOTES

Fiddlewoods prefer climates that are tropical to warm, but they will grow in cooler gardens if protected from frost while young. The trees are best in full sun and in well-drained soil that is enriched with organic matter. In the tropics, the flowers may be followed by berry-like fruits.

CUPRESSUS SPECIES & CULTIVARS
CYPRESS

The trees of the genus *Cupressus* are sometimes called the 'true cypresses', to distinguish them from other conifers sharing their common name. Cypresses deserve distinction. Their ancestry goes back to prehistoric times and even in cultivation there are individual trees, such as in Europe, which are many hundreds of years old. The genus includes the Kashmir cypress (*Cupressus cashmeriana*); the Mediterranean cypress or pencil pine (*C. sempervirens*); the Bhutan cypress (*C. torulosa*), from the Himalayas; and the Monterey cypress (*C. macrocarpa*), which is almost extinct in its natural habitat and survives in two precious stands along the Californian coast.

Cypresses have featured in gardening since at least Classical times. Now, as well as the species, there are many ornamental cultivars, including those with dense habits for hedging; columnar or tapered forms; pendulous foliage; or colourful leaves tinted blue-grey or dusted with yellow-gold. But, despite the cypresses' long and distinguished history, the most commonly grown form in gardens today is an upstart.

The Leyland cypress, x *Cupressocyparis*, is a hybrid of two genera (an uncommon occurrence in botany), and its parents are reputedly the Alaskan cedar (*Chamaecyparis nootkatensis*)

Cypresses are ancient, but have long been adapted to gardens. The Monterey cypress (left) is often used in hedges. 'Castlewellan' (above) is a cultivar of the Leyland cypress.

In gardens, cypresses are favoured in formal styles and hedging, but they can also be crafted into designs that display their creative characteristics.

and the Monterey cypress. Since it first appeared in an English nursery in the 1880s, the Leyland itself has been re-created in several cultivars and the hybrid has eclipsed other cypresses with its vigour and versatility.

GROWING NOTES

Cypresses, with their diverse origins and many cultivars, will adapt to climates from warm to cold. They are best in full sun, and except for the Kashmir cypress are tolerant of windy and exposed conditions. They prefer well-drained soil, though not necessarily rich; and regular watering until established. Only some forms suit clipping and hedging; others should be allowed to develop their natural shapes.

CYATHEA & DICKSONIA SPECIES
TREE FERNS

Tree ferns bring the atmosphere of an ancient rainforest to the garden with their finely leaved fronds, such as *Cyathea rebeccae* (above).

Tree ferns bring a unique atmosphere to the garden and evoke an air of antipodean forests, ancient and lush. Looking up at the sky, at the world, through the leaves of tree ferns is a magical experience, and watching their fronds unfurl is to witness the birth of something special. Tree ferns entice us to spend a moment in rainforest time.

Both *Dicksonia* and *Cyathea*, relations that share the common name of tree fern, occur naturally only in Australia, New Zealand and some islands of the South Pacific. These tree ferns, however, are very adaptable to various climates and so they are enjoyed in gardens worldwide.

Dicksonia antarctica, endemic to Australia and New Zealand, and *D. fibrosa*, of New Zealand, are two of the most commonly grown tree ferns. They adapt to frost-free climates, and are very marketable: a mature tree can be cut at the base and the

Many of the tree ferns, such as *Cyathea* species (opposite and below) and *Dicksonia antarctica* (left), are adaptable to a range of garden conditions including cooler climates and containers.

trunk transplanted (although sadly the original plant will not re-grow). The *Cyathea* species are less commercially minded and can be propagated only by spores, but they are among the few ferns that tolerate cold. *Cyathea australis* and *C. cooperi* are tall-growing species with light canopies, and they are especially adaptable to garden cultivation.

GROWING NOTES

All tree ferns prefer shaded, sheltered conditions with moist rich soil—in their native rainforests, they are understorey plants. Hot, direct sun or light frost may burn the leaves but the plant usually survives, albeit with a slightly tattered canopy. Depending on the species, they can reach 15 metres (45 ft) in height, but tree ferns can also be grown in large containers and enclosed garden spaces, mingling well with palms, other ferns and tropical plants.

DRACAENA DRACO
DRAGON'S BLOOD TREE

The dragon's blood tree is a feature of a lifetime and the jewel in any garden.

The dragon's blood tree is a compelling arboreal creature, and most gardeners are unlikely to forget a meeting with *Dracaena draco*. It's about as dramatic as a plant can get, with an enormous crown of spiky rosettes atop thick upswept limbs, and, when cut, the tree oozes with blood-red sap (giving rise to the many magical beliefs that surround it). Native to the Canary Islands, the dragon's blood tree is remarkably adaptable too. Extremely long-lived and slow-growing, with new branches produced every decade or so, the dragon's blood tree will also grow in a container for many years.

GROWING NOTES

The dragon's blood tree will grow in frost-free climates from cool to tropical. They require full sun, open aspects and very well drained soils (preferably sandy or gravelly). Water regularly to establish, after which the tree only needs deep watering when the soil dries out. These plants are easy to grow, but prone to root rot. They can be grown from seed, sown in early spring, and from cuttings, though these are rare as they disfigure the parent tree.

EUCALYPTUS & CORYMBIA SPECIES
GUM TREES

Many gum trees are ideal for gardens, such as the red-flowering types (above); the spotted gum, *Corymbia maculata* (below) and the scribbly gum, *Eucalyptus haemastoma* (opposite).

The gum tree is the definitive living feature of the Australian landscape. However, there are actually two genera, *Eucalyptus* and *Corymbia*, which stand under the banner of gum tree, with more than 600 species across Australia but also in New Guinea and the Philippines. The gum trees have been known to horticulture since Sir Joseph Banks reputedly coined the term in the late 1770s. Among the best known are the lemon-scented gum, *Corymbia citriodora*, which has shining pale grey bark and aromatic leaves; the red-flowering gum, *C. ficifolia*; and the Argyle apple, *Eucalyptus cinerea*, the favourite form of floristry, with its rounded juvenile leaves of silvery-blue.

GROWING NOTES

Gum trees originate in diverse habitats, and there are species to suit climates from tropical to cold. Most prefer open aspects, full sun and well-drained soil, although some also grow in waterlogged conditions. The trees range in height from about 6 metres (18 ft) to almost 100 metres (300 ft), with the mountain ash, *E. regnans*, being the tallest of their kind.

FICUS SPECIES
FIG

The figs are an influential group in the plant kingdom, with more than 800 species of trees, shrubs and climbers distributed across warm parts of the world. Some figs are also very significant to humankind—like the common fig, *Ficus carica* (see page 438); the banyan, *F. benghalensis*, sacred in its native India; and the bo, *F. religiosa*, which many believe is the tree under which Buddha found enlightenment. Most *Ficus* trees will grow too large for gardens, with their famous buttressed roots or stranglers. However, the genus also includes popular trees for pots and indoors, including the weeping fig, *F. benjamina*; the Indian rubber tree, *F. elastica*; and the fiddleleaf, *F. lyrata*, from Africa.

Most fig trees grow into buttressed giants which would engulf ordinary gardens; however, many of them are also favoured as houseplants and in pots.

GROWING NOTES
Most figs will grow in frost-free climates, but are suitable only for the largest gardens. Take care even with outdoor potted specimens, as their roots will quickly escape their containers if placed directly on the ground. Indoors, figs reign, and few trees are so forgiving or adaptable.

LAURUS NOBILIS
BAY

Bay trees are evergreens with naturally appealing habits; however, many trees in cultivation are formally clipped and they are also favoured subjects of topiary.

The bay is one of the most iconic trees in our collective history. Its species name, *nobilis*, means notable; it gives a common name, the laurel, to victory, award and distinction; it is considered a king among herbs; ancient civilisations knew it; and the Greek god Apollo is rarely pictured unaccessorised by his sacred leaves. The bay is more than tree, it is an ideal.

In the garden, the bay ranks among the finest of ornamentals. Deservingly, the trees are often featured as central plants in herb gardens, formal designs and parterres; and bays are also splendid in containers. They can be trained into standards, grown as hedges, or tightly clipped in topiary—an artform which has favoured the bay for hundreds of years.

In cultivation, *Laurus nobilis*, also known as the sweet bay, rarely reaches its wild dimensions of 10–20 metres (30–60 ft) in height and width at maturity. The growth of garden trees is slow and their size more sedate, usually around 6–8 metres

The intrinsic formality of the bay is ideal for clipping. The trees also have fragrant creamy flowers in spring, which may be followed by green berries that ripen purple.

(18–24 ft) tall. Evergreen and long-lived, bay trees can naturally develop multi-stems and bushy, shrub-like habits, or form single trunks with broad canopies. Bay trees are easy to train, and even when clipped their maintenance is more like a privilege than a chore.

GROWING NOTES

Bay trees can be grown in all garden climates except the very cold or tropical. The plants are best in full sun, especially those used in hedging or topiary, but will tolerate some shade. The soil must be well drained, though not necessarily rich. Water regularly to establish, after which the trees are tolerant of dry conditions. Potted plants should be well fed and watered to promote good growth.

LICUALA SPECIES
FAN PALM

Many plants are called fan palms, but most gardeners consider the *Licuala* genus to be the luxury-model of these. Its fronds are spectacular and at the upper end of the fan-palm market—enormous and circular, gathered in numerous perfect pleats. Of the species, *Licuala grandis* is the most commonly grown. Like most of the fan palms, it is naturally found in the understoreys of tropical rainforests, where it grows to only 2–4 metres (6–12 ft) in height. Also widely cultivated is *L. ramsayii*, which can grow to 15 metres (45 ft) in ideal conditions, with a narrow trunk and fronds up to 1 metre (3 ft) wide.

The pleated circular fronds of the fan palms, such as *Licuala ramsayii* (left and below) and *L. pumila* (above), are spectacular in colour, form and size.

GROWING NOTES
Fan palms require tropical and very warm climates, but can also be grown in glasshouses in cooler areas. They prefer shade or dappled shade, shelter from strong wind, and humid environments. The soil should be well drained and enriched with aged organic matter. Water regularly throughout the growing season. Finished fronds may be removed, cut cleanly close to the trunk, to keep the palms tidy.

LIVISTONA CHINENSIS
CHINESE FAN PALM

The broad fronds of the Chinese fan palm are deeply split at the tips into long wispy sections, giving the canopy its distinctly dripping appearance. Widely grown in parks in tropical and warm regions, *Livistona chinensis* is very adaptable to gardens, even growing for many years in containers. In ideal conditions, the Chinese fan palm can reach 8–10 metres (25–30 ft) in height, but in gardens it is slow-growing to about 4–5 metres (12–15 ft). Even in younger trees where the leaves can hang to the ground, the foliage crown is large and spectacular—a cascade of fronds that gives the plant its alternative common name of fountain palm.

GROWING NOTES

The Chinese fan palm adapts to climates from tropical to quite cool, and will withstand light frost in winter. The plants grow in full sun or part shade, but require protection from strong wind which wrecks the appearance of their leaves. The soil should be well drained but not necessarily rich. Water regularly to establish the plants; however, mature trees are fairly tolerant of drought.

The cascading appearance of the Chinese fan palm is formed by broad fronds with deeply divided, ribbon-like leaf tips.

LOPHOSTEMON CONFERTUS
BRUSH BOX

Evergreen trees with naturally attractive canopies never lose their appeal with discerning gardeners. The brush box is one of the most elegant and stately of these, with variegated cultivars that add colour to its charms. The species, *Lophostemon confertus* (syn. *Tristania conferta*), is native to eastern Australia, where it can grow to more than 40 metres (120 ft) in height. In gardens, the tree rarely exceeds 20 metres (60 ft) and its canopy forms into a shapely, conical, broad dome. The variegated cultivars only grow to 10 metres (30 ft) and are more tapered: 'Variegata', with cream and green leaves, and 'Perth Gold', with gold and green.

GROWING NOTES

The brush box is best in tropical and warm climates, but will tolerate cooler temperatures in frost-free and sheltered positions. Full sun is required to form dense canopies and to keep variegations brightly coloured. Water well in summer to prevent excessive leaf loss. On variegated cultivars, remove plain green growth if it appears.

The fanned arrangement of the leaves of brush box is enhanced by variegations. These smaller-growing cultivars have naturally elegant and dense canopies.

PICEA SPECIES & CULTIVARS
SPRUCE

Spruces are distinguished by their needle-like leaves, arranged in whorls, and their pendent cones; the Himalayan spruce (above and opposite) forms an impressive pyramid-shaped canopy.

The spruce trees are among the largest of the conifers. In their natural habitats, they can grow into enormous columns or form giant pyramids, 50 metres (150 ft) tall or more. Among them are the commonly known *Picea abies*, from Norway and northern Europe, which some believe is the prototype Christmas tree; the Himalayan spruce, *P. smithiana*; the white spruce, *P. glauca*, from Canada; and the Colorado spruce, *P. pungens*, and its famous blue-leaf forms. There are, however, also many spruce cultivars which are smaller growing and ideal for gardens. Some of the dwarf types rarely exceed 1–3 metres (3–9 ft) in height, and are suitable for growing in containers.

GROWING NOTES

Spruces are best in cool to cold, moist climates; however, some cultivars will grow in temperate gardens. They require full sun and open aspects, although they prefer some afternoon shade in warmer regions. The soil should be deep and well drained. Water generously to establish the trees, and during dry warm seasons. Do not allow potted specimens to dry out.

Pine trees are the archetypal conifers, and many species have ornamental assets. *Pinus patula* (opposite and left) is known for long needles; *P. roxburghii* (below) features textured bark.

PINUS SPECIES & CULTIVARS
PINE

The pines aren't just the most famous of the conifers, they are among the best known of all trees in the world. There are, in fact, more than 90 species of pines in the genus *Pinus*, sometimes referred to as the 'true pines', and they occur throughout the northern hemisphere, with one species from Indonesia. The pines include some very significant trees, valuable for timber, paper, resin (which becomes turpentine) and cones (which bear pine nuts). The pines are also the oldest living creatures on earth—the bristlecone pine (*Pinus aristata*) has representatives in California that science has dated at more than 4,000 years old.

While most of the pine species become too large for gardens and so remain in the province of parks or forestry, some are

The pines are a very adaptable group and can be grown as feature trees in large gardens, for example the Scots pine, *Pinus sylvestris* (right), and *P. canariensis* (opposite). Some will grow in rockeries and containers as well.

ornamentally grown. The Mexican pine, *P. patula*, grows to 10–15 metres (30–45 ft) in height, in a pyramidal shape, with pendulous foliage that forms a weeping canopy. The Aleppo pine, *P. halepensis*, is popular too, being adaptable and growing to 10 metres (30 ft) tall. The dwarf mountain pine, *P. mugo*, is also favoured: it is naturally short, but also has cultivars that are ideal for containers, small gardens and rockeries.

GROWING NOTES

Pines have such diverse origins that there are species to suit all gardening climates, from very cold to tropical. They generally prefer full sun and open aspects; however, pines from cool, moist climates will require some shelter and shade in warm gardens. Pine trees will grow in exposed situations and they make excellent windbreaks. Water trees regularly to establish them. Potted specimens should not be allowed to dry out.

SABAL PALMETTO
PALMETTO

Although its large fan-leaved canopy is outstanding, the palmetto is also admired for its trunk—magnificently broad at maturity and encased by old sheaths that are elegantly interwoven. Originating from south-eastern North America, often in coastal areas, the palmetto is very adaptable to a range of climates and can be fast-growing and long-lived. Although it can reach 25 metres (75 ft) in height in its natural habitat, this palm is usually much smaller in gardens. Its fronds are huge, deeply divided and stand out from the trunk with a slight but distinctive twist.

GROWING NOTES

Palmettos are best in tropical and warm climates and thrive in high humidity. However, these palms also adapt to cooler gardens and will even tolerate light frost once established. They grow in full sun or part shade, and prefer well-drained soil, on the sandy side. Young plants require regular watering, but mature palmettos will withstand fairly long periods of drought. These palms are well suited to coastal conditions.

The huge and deeply divided fronds of palmetto create a great impact, but the mature trunk, encased by old leaf bases, is a fine feature too.

SEQUOIA & SEQUOIADENDRON
REDWOODS

Few gardeners will ever get the chance to plant a redwood, for these are the largest trees in the world. For most gardeners, it's enough to have met (or hugged) one, and many have made pilgrimages to the national parks of California to pay homage to these great trees. *Sequoia sempervirens*, the Californian redwood, claims the title of the world's biggest tree (the size of trees is measured in volume not height); and the current winner is an individual named General Sherman in the Sierra Nevada Mountains (mecca of the ancient giant redwoods). However, its cousin, *Sequoiadendron giganteum*, the giant redwood, holds the record for yielding the most timber. Closely related, with only one species in each genus, both these redwoods are also remarkably long-lived—with the trees growing for 1,000 years or more.

Although the tree is suitable only for large gardens, the Californian redwood, with its tiered and columnar habit, is a memorable feature.

GROWING NOTES

Redwoods are suitable only for large gardens where the trees can become the momentous features that they are. They prefer cool, moist climates; however, the Californian redwood will adapt to warmer regions as well. The soil must be deep and well drained. The trees require regular rainfall or watering.

TAXUS BACCATA
YEW

The yew trees have been cultivated for thousands of years, yet in gardens they are rarely seen in their natural coniferous forms. Instead, most gardeners know yews as doyens of hedging and topiary. They were among the first plants to be used in these horticultural ways, and there are some individuals in Europe that have been continuously grown, and clipped, for centuries. With slow-growing and long-lived habits and dense needle-like leaves, yews may be trained into perfectly uniform hedges or fantastical shapes—cones, spirals, balls, obelisks or whimsical creatures—limited only by the gardener's imagination. The plants may also be grown in rockeries and pots. There are many cultivars of *Taxus baccata*, the common yew, including yellow-leaved forms.

Set in densely packed spirals, the flat, needle-like leaves of yews have been made famous in the perfection of hedges and topiary.

GROWING NOTES
Yew trees are best in cool to cold climates, and very tolerant of wind and frost. The plants prefer open aspects; full sun, for dense, even growth; and well-drained soil enriched with organic matter. Water regularly, especially in dry warm seasons. To create shapes, prune little but often. Note that yews are poisonous to humans and animals.

THUJA SPECIES & CULTIVARS

THUJA

There are only five species of *Thuja* but they include one of the most significant conifers—the western red cedar, *Thuja plicata*, the behemoth of the timber industry—and some of their best ornamental forms. Much smaller than the western reds, the decorative species of *Thuja* are sometimes known as the arbor-vitaes and include *T. occidentalis*, from northern America, and *T. orientalis*, from China and Japan. Both of these species have numerous cultivars. These vary in form, from bun-shaped or conical to columnar, and leaf colour, including purplish, iridescent green or gold. With their great range, the ornamental thujas are very popular, but they are also among the easiest of conifers to grow in gardens.

GROWING NOTES

The ornamental thujas adapt to a range of climates from warm to cold, but prefer cool, moist environments. *T. orientalis* and its cultivars also grow in subtropical and tropical climates; however, the golden-leaved varieties may struggle. All thujas are best in well-drained soil and open aspects. They require full sun to develop dense growth and foliage colours.

The thujas, including the western red cedar (left and top), have distinctive feathery sprays of foliage. 'Rheingold' (above) is a popular cultivar of *Thuja occidentalis*.

The windmill palms thrive in both cool and warm climates, but also tolerate dry conditions once the plants are established.

TRACHYCARPUS FORTUNEI
WINDMILL PALM

Palms that thrive in cool climates and can tolerate a touch of frost are hard to come by—the windmill palm, or Chusan palm, is one of these treasures. The species *Trachycarpus fortunei*, from China, was introduced to European gardeners in the 19th century (collected by the plant hunter, Robert Fortune, of course) and has remained the most popular of the genus. This windmill palm has a solitary trunk clothed in the rough remains of old leaf sheaths, giving it a distinctive texture and rich colour. The deeply divided fan-shaped fronds stand out from the trunk, enhancing the rounded crown of foliage. Although they can eventually reach 12 metres (36 ft) in height, these palms are fairly slow to mature, and they grow in containers for years.

GROWING NOTES

Windmill palms will grow in cool to warm climates, however, they are unsuitable for the tropics. They are best in full sun (but also adapt to part shade), and require well-drained soil. Remove the old fronds to keep the plants tidy, or enjoy them as part of the palm's natural display.

WASHINGTONIA SPECIES
COTTON PALM

There are only two species in this genus, named after the US President, George Washington, but the cotton palms are among the most widely grown of their kind throughout the world. They adapt to a range of climates, and are outstanding in parks and streetscapes, but are suitable for home gardens too. *Washingtonia filifera* grows to 15 metres (45 ft) in height and is distinguished by the cotton-like threads on its huge fan-shaped fronds. *W. robusta,* also known as the skyduster, can reach 20 metres (60 ft) or more, and doesn't have threads on its mature leaves. The finished fronds of *Washingtonia* can also become a feature of the palm—forming a layered skirt enclosing the trunk all the way to the ground.

GROWING NOTES

Cotton palms prefer tropical to temperate climates, and suit both coastal and inland conditions. *W. filifera* also adapts to cooler gardens if protected from heavy frost. These palms will tolerate full sun, even as tender young plants. The soil must be well drained. Water regularly to establish; once mature these palms are very resistant to drought.

The fronds of the cotton palm are striking when these plants are young. These trouble-free palms can grow to towering heights at maturity.

cycads

In the botanical world, the cycads stand alone. Although they look similar to palms, produce seeds like flowering plants, and can even be termed perennial, cycads are unique. They have no close relations in the plant kingdom. The cycads' ancestry goes back about 250 million years, earning these extraordinary plants the title of living fossils.

Cycads are evergreen

and dramatic year round.

Clockwise from top left:

the sago palm; *Zamia*

cone; cardboard plants;

the burrawang.

Cycads are distinguished from all other living plants by a set of unusual botanical features. These include pinnate leaves, with numerous leaflets on either side of a central rib, that are spirally arranged in crowns, and stout, thick stems (trunks). Another rare characteristic is the cycads' 'cones', which are their reproductive structures, with the male and female types borne on separate plants. The plants are also defined by the presence of certain toxins, such as cycasin, especially in the cycad's seeds.

Currently, there are 11 known genera of cycads, with about 250 species between them, distributed throughout the tropical and subtropical parts of the world. Sadly, even though some of these species have been around for 50 million years or more, they are nearing extinction in the wild. In gardens, however, it's a different story, and, with increasing appreciation for their uniqueness, cycads are on the rise.

The most commonly grown of all the cycads is *Cycas revoluta*, the sago palm, which originates in Japan and belongs to the oldest of the current cycad families. It has a distinctive crown of arching fronds, composed of narrow leaflets and spreading up to 2 metres (6 ft) wide. The plants are very slow growing, eventually reaching an impressive 3 metres (9 ft) in height, and capable of suckering at the base to create a dramatic clump.

Although they are among
the most ancient plants on
earth, cycads have
adapted amazingly well
to modern life. The
cardboard plant thrives in
warm gardens, but also
in pots and indoors.

The cardboard plant, also known as the cardboard palm, *Zamia furfuracea*, is another popular cycad. With dramatic fronds of leathery, rigid leaflets, the plant grows to about 1 metre (3 ft) in height, and its crown may be twice as wide. Although threatened in its native habitat of eastern Mexico, this cycad has been remarkably adaptable to urban environments and is widely cultivated. Some of the *Zamia* species, including *Z. furfuracea*, also cross readily between themselves, producing hybrids in the wild, and in gardens too.

Other cycads which are ornamentally grown include the genus *Encephalartos*, endemic to southern Africa, which has sculptural fronds and colourful cones. Also decorative are the Australian species, *Lepidozamia peroffskyana*, the scaly zamia, which can grow 7 metres (21 ft) in height and has glossy leaflets, and *Macrozamia communis*, the burrawang, with fronds that can be 2 metres (6 ft) long.

Any cycad in the garden brings an aura of rarity and timelessness, but also a sense of drama. Cycads are naturally evocative and exciting in garden designs, as individual specimens, in jungle-like understoreys, or in landscaped groups. Ironically, they look ultra-modern, too, and are ideal for minimalist or architectural styles. Many cycads will also grow in pots—in courtyards, on balconies, as bonsai, even indoors, where they create outstanding displays.

Cycads are distinguished botanically and in the garden by their unusual features. Clockwise from top left: cardboard plant leaflets; red seeds of *Encephalartos*; whorled leaves of *Zamia*; trunk of the scaly zamia.

GROWING NOTES

Many of the cycads, as their history shows, are incredibly adaptable plants which thrive in cultivation. Most of the common forms prefer tropical to warm climates. Some also grow in cool gardens and will tolerate light frost, and the sago palm can handle quite cold conditions.

In general, cycads will grow in full sun to part shade, but their foliage is better in bright situations. The soil should be well drained and preferably enriched with aged organic matter. In containers, use a good quality potting mix that is light but retains moisture. Water the plants regularly and deeply throughout spring and summer, but less in winter. All cycads are very long-lived and slow-growing, and once established they require little maintenance. An organic mulch is appreciated by most cycads, and old fronds may be removed, if desired, to keep the plants tidy.

Mature cycads can develop impressive cones, but seeds are only produced if plants of both sexes are present. Cycad seeds are toxic unless specially treated and should not be eaten.

Cycads look exotic, but these plants can be very easy to grow. The sago palm, *Cycas revoluta*, is a popular species for cooler gardens.

deciduous trees

Deciduous trees influence our garden designs, but they also bring the seasons into our gardening lives. Their foliage colour, which occurs before the leaves are cast, is one of autumn's highlights, and they are the garden's architectural features of winter. In spring and summer, the trees' lush leaf canopies bring welcome shade, and sometimes they bear flower or fruit as well.

The changing colours of deciduous foliage is one of the garden's seasonal highlights. This page: A woodland-style grove featuring deciduous trees, including maples. Previous pages: A red-leaved cultivar of Japanese maple.

Many trees and shrubs are deciduous, and some can be valuable for fruit or flowers, as seen in other chapters. This chapter features deciduous trees that are renowned for their autumnal foliage colours, but also for their winter forms. By nature, deciduous trees are diverse and their seasonal characteristics vary depending on where they grow—an essential part of their charm.

Deciduous trees bring the seasons into garden designs. Left: Many of these trees have leaves brighter than their flowers. Right: Red winter branches of *Acer palmatum* 'Senkaki'. Following pages: An avenue of deciduous trees.

In gardens, maples have many charms. 'Senkaki' (below) is a cultivar of the Japanese maple. The leaves of the sugar maple (opposite) blaze with autumn colour.

ACER SPECIES & CULTIVARS
MAPLE

Few trees are as well known as the maple. For thousands of years, it has been cultivated in China and Japan, where many species of *Acer* originate; maples were planted around ancient Buddhist temples and are intrinsic to Zen gardens. In north America and Europe, where maples are also found, they are similarly elite. But, unlike other iconic trees grown for flowers, timber or fruit, the maple is famous for its leaves.

The maple leaf is distinctive—typically palmate and deeply lobed. And, even though some *Acer* species have undivided foliage and other plant types share the pointy shape, the maple is the archetype of starry leaves. Most maples are deciduous, and few plants can rival their jewel-like autumn colours, for which the maples are renowned. However, these trees are also

The Japanese maple has many forms; some are centuries-old, including those with dissected leaves (right) or purple-red foliage in spring (below). *Acer negundo* (opposite) has oval leaflets instead of starry leaves.

much admired for their spring and summer canopies, which hover around the spreading branches like clouds of leaf.

Of all the ornamental species, the Japanese maple, *Acer palmatum*, is the most commonly grown and has an astounding range of more than 200 cultivars. Other popular species include the sugar maple, *A. saccharum*, which is the source of maple syrup, and the trident maple, *A. buergerianum* (syn. *A. trifidum*), with triangular-shaped leaves.

GROWING NOTES

Most of the maples are best in cool to cold, moist climates; however, some are adaptable to warmer gardens. The Japanese maple grows (and colours) well in more temperate regions. The trees prefer full sun, with shelter from strong wind but in warm climates they require afternoon shade. The soil should be fairly rich and well drained. Water regularly in spring and summer, and generously during dry seasons.

BETULA SPECIES
BIRCH

The birch is a magical kind of tree. In its native lands, throughout the northern hemisphere, the birch is a significant feature in legends, history and lore. All over the world, gardeners know the tree's power too. It is symbolic. When you plant a birch, a garden is born.

As single features or in close-knit groves, along avenues and in great stands, birch trees are enchanting in garden designs, and in all seasons as well. They have graceful deciduous habits, in cultivation reaching 15–20 metres (45–60 ft) tall, with lacy canopies that cast an airy dappled shade. In early spring, the bare branches are festooned with catkins. However, birches are more often appreciated for their delicately shaped leaves— bright green in spring and summer, and glittering gold in autumn—and also for their bark, which is outstanding in metallic tones or when clothing their trunks in scrolls.

Although many species of birch are ornamental, the silver birch, *Betula pendula*, remains the most popular. It is very

An arboreal legend, the silver birch (opposite and above) has been cultivated for centuries and remains the most popular species in gardens.

Birch trees, with their graceful habits and lacy canopies, bring an air of enchantment to gardens. *Betula maximowicziana* (below) features bark that is particularly beautiful.

adaptable in gardens and easy to grow, with a range of cultivars—including the cut-leaf birch, *B. pendula* 'Dalecarlica', and the weeping form 'Youngii'—which further extend this great tree's versatility. However, for something really special, there are also birches with bark of otherworldly beauty, such as the species *B. maximowicziana* and the variety of the Himalayan birch, *B. utilis* var. *jacquemontii*.

GROWING NOTES

Most of the birch trees prefer cool to cold, moist climates but some will adapt to warmer regions, too. They are best in open positions, with full sun, but in warm gardens they require afternoon shade. The soil should be well drained and enriched with plenty of organic matter. Water generously in spring and summer, especially in warm-climate gardens.

CORYLUS SPECIES & CULTIVARS
HAZEL

The contorted habit of the corkscrew hazel is best appreciated in winter; catkins (male flowers) will form on the bare branches, before leaves appear in spring.

Most of the hazels in cultivation are grown for their edible nuts and useful ornamental habits, including the hazelnut or filbert, *Corylus maxima*, and the common hazel or cobnut, *C. avellana*. But not 'Contorta'. This naturally occurring variety of *C. avellana* is daringly different. Its branches and stems are bent, curled and twisted—a feature favoured by gardeners and floral artists alike, and which gives the tree its common name of corkscrew hazel (although it is sometimes also called the crazy filbert). Corkscrews, like other common hazels, are multi-stemmed, growing to 4–5 metres (12–15 ft) in height and width, and, while they make excellent screens, windbreaks or hedges, they are usually appreciated just for being beautiful and bizarre.

GROWING NOTES

Corkscrew hazels prefer cool climates, or those with hot, dry summers and cool, wet winters. The trees require full sun, and like well-drained soil but aren't fussy. They are very tolerant of exposed conditions and strong winds. Corkscrew hazels may be planted in containers, to create fascinating potted features.

The common beech is a feature of natural landscapes in Europe, but has also developed garden traits over the centuries.

FAGUS SYLVATICA
COMMON BEECH

Often known as the English beech, the common beech is actually endemic to many parts of Europe. From the wild windswept stands and ancient woodlands of its native habitats, *Fagus sylvatica* has come a long way. The common beech has been in cultivation for centuries, as a feature tree and in hedging, parterres and topiary, and has a range of decorative forms. Famously, there's the copper beech, a variety called *purpurea*, with deep burgundy leaves and rich red autumn colour, and the weeping beech, var. *pendula*, which has pendulous branches and a cascading canopy. There are also many named cultivars, including 'Zlatia', which has bright yellow foliage, as well as rarer forms with variegated leaves.

GROWING NOTES

Although the beeches are adaptable, they are best in cool to cold climates. They require full sun, and the purple-foliage forms won't produce good colour without it. However, some of the pale-leaf cultivars do prefer part shade. The soil should be well drained and fairly rich. If shaping them, beech trees should be trimmed in summer.

FRAXINUS SPECIES & CULTIVARS
ASH

Although the ash trees were initially valued for their timber, which is tough and smooth-grained, they've also found fame ornamentally. Originating throughout the northern hemisphere, there are about 60 species in the genus *Fraxinus*, and many are cultivated in gardens and parks, as well as commercially for wood. Ash trees are deciduous, and distinguished by their pinnate leaves, with numerous paired leaflets—creating their trademark fluttering canopies which in autumn shimmer gold, bronze and copper.

While most are naturally tall—such as the white ash, *Fraxinus americana*, and European ash, *F. excelsior*, which can reach 30–40 metres (90–120 ft) in height—the cultivated forms are generally smaller, and preferred in garden designs. The golden ash, a cultivar 'Aurea' of *F. excelsior*, is one of the most popular, with bright yellow autumn foliage; so too is the claret ash *F.* 'Raywood', which grows to about 6–10 metres (18–30 ft) and has seasonally coloured, deep red leaves.

In gardens, the ash is a graceful feature tree. One of the most popular ornamental forms is the golden ash (left), *Fraxinus excelsior* 'Aurea'.

The typically fluttering canopy of the ash tree is created by fine leaflets. In summer the crown casts rippling shade, and in autumn it shimmers richly with colour.

GROWING NOTES

Ash trees are very adaptable to a range of climates, from warm to cool; however, they are not suitable for extremely cold areas and the tropics. Most of the species and cultivars prefer regions with high rainfall, while the desert ash, *F. oxycarpa*, as its name suggests, can handle the driest climatic conditions as well as drought. Many ash trees are also tolerant of pollution, which makes them very suitable for urban designs and avenues. The plants prefer full sun and deep, well-drained soil; they benefit from regular watering during the growing season.

GINKGO BILOBA
GINKGO

The ginkgo tree is a privilege to know. Its ancestors go back at least 200 million years, making ginkgoes older than most pines and cycads, but the genus of only one species, originating in China, has long been extinct in the wild. Yet the ginkgo survives, and thrives, in cultivation. It has been grown for centuries around Buddhist temples in China and Japan (this is reputed to have saved the tree from extinction); it features in streetscapes, being extremely tolerant of pollution, and in parks; it is revered in gardens; and the ginkgo has remarkable medicinal uses too.

Incredibly long-lived, with individual specimens in Asia that are many hundreds of years old, the ginkgo tree can reach 20–30 metres (60–90 ft) at maturity, and may spread into a giant with an enormous girth. Some cultivars have narrow,

Ginkgoes are botanically unique, and among the oldest of existing species in the plant kingdom; the trees have survived extinction by thriving in cultivation.

The ginkgo is also known as the maidenhair tree. Its fan-shaped leaves are light green in spring and summer, and in autumn the tree's entire canopy becomes golden.

upright habits or ascending branches, while others have broad canopies that tend to weep. The ginkgo's leaves are beautiful and unique. Fan-shaped, with wavy edges and a soft leathery texture, the leaves are prehistorically designed and so they are resistant to 'modern' pests and diseases.

GROWING NOTES

Ginkgoes are very adaptable and will grow in climates from warm to cool. They require full sun, with shelter from strong wind. The trees are best in deep, moist soil, but will tolerate poorer conditions. In their early years, they may be grown in large pots, and ginkgoes are also suitable for bonsai. Water regularly to establish the plants, but also during dry seasons. Ginkgo trees may be male or female, with only female trees producing fruit (this usually occurs after about 30 years).

GLEDITSIA TRIACANTHOS
HONEY LOCUST

Originating in North America, the honey locust is one of autumn's famously golden trees, with its generous canopy of ferny leaves glittering bright yellow. However, most gardeners bypass the species, *Gleditsia triacanthos*, with its trunk covered in savage thorns and a mature height of more than 30 metres (90 ft), and choose one of its cultivars instead. These include the thornless *G. triacanthos* var. *inermis*, favoured for its lack of aggressive parts; 'Sunburst', with bright yellow-green foliage and a height of about 10 metres (30 ft); and 'Ruby Lace', with reddish-purple leaves.

GROWING NOTES

Honey locusts will grow in a range of climates, from cool to subtropical. The foliage colour is best in full sun, but there is also the cultivar 'Shademaster' which grows in part shade. These trees prefer a well-drained, deep soil, although they aren't overly fussy about quality. They are resistant to pollution, and fairly tolerant of drought once established.

'Sunburst' (left) is a cultivar with light green foliage in spring and summer that turns bright yellow in autumn. Long dark seed pods decorate the honey locust's bare branches.

JUGLANS REGIA
WALNUT

Although the walnut is commercially grown for its nuts, in the garden it is a monument, with incredible presence in designs. *Juglans regia*, of possibly Persian origin but of English fame, grows very slowly, may take 20 years to start producing crops, and can live for 200 or more. The species grows tall, 15–20 metres (45–60 ft) in height, and equally broad; though its American relation, *J. nigra*, is taller still. The leaves of the walnut tree are large and compound, with leaflets up to 15 cm (6 inches) long, creating a tremendous canopy that casts a sea of summer shade. Deciduous, the foliage falls in autumn to reveal, by winter, the walnut's magnificent form.

The walnut is a tree for large gardens and parks, where it can grow unrestricted at leisure and eventually become a venerable beauty.

GROWING NOTES

Walnut trees are best in cool and temperate climates. They require full sun, a lot of space, and deep, well-drained soil. Young trees and those grown for crops should be watered regularly throughout spring and summer. Avoid pruning. There are many cultivars of *J. regia* available, and those which are touted as disease-resistant should be preferred.

KOELREUTERIA SPECIES
GOLDEN RAIN TREE

According to legend, the leaves of the golden rain trees inspired the willow pattern featured on chinaware, such is the influential beauty of their foliage. Originating in China and western Asia, golden rain trees, as their history suggests, are very ornamental. They grow 10–15 metres (30–45 ft) in height, with a wispy, slightly weeping crown that is formed by long, compound leaves of perfectly ovate leaflets. In autumn, the foliage becomes like gold filigree. The best-known species is *Koelreuteria paniculata*, which has yellow spring flowers in panicles up to 30 cm (1 ft) long, followed by papery lantern-shaped fruits which, for months, will also decorate the tree.

GROWING NOTES

Golden rain trees grow well in cool to warm climates, but they are best in areas where winters are cold and summers are hot and dry. The plants prefer full sun, open aspects and well-drained soil that is enriched with organic matter. Water regularly to establish the trees, after which they are quite tolerant of dry periods.

The golden rain tree has a distinctive leaf shape and autumn colour, but its refined habit also adds elegance to designs.

LIQUIDAMBAR SPECIES & CULTIVARS
LIQUIDAMBAR

The liquidambar has earned its place among the doyens of deciduous trees. In gardens and parks, along avenues and in cities throughout the world, the liquidambars—with their canopies of starry leaves bursting into seasonal tones of yellow, orange, purple, bronze and red—have become symbolic of autumnal beauty.

Apart from their brilliant autumn colour, liquidambars are majestic trees. They grow tall, about 30 metres (90 ft) in height, and develop splendid pyramid-shaped canopies that may be 10 metres (30 ft) wide. The trees are reliable, too, and adapt to a range of conditions, producing their foliage display in warm climates as well as cool.

Ornamentally, the northern American species *Liquidambar styraciflua*, or sweet gum, is the most commonly grown of these trees. This liquidambar is known for its star-shaped leaves, with 5–7 acute lobes on each, its spiky round fruits, and the corky texture of its young branches. It has many

Liquidambars are very adaptable to garden conditions and designs. They are one of the best deciduous trees for brilliant autumn colour in warm climates.

The liquidambars are renowned for their beautiful leaves and canopies; their autumn colours can vary from tree to tree, even when they are planted together.

cultivars, including 'Golden Treasure', a dwarf form with variegated cream and green leaves. Also ornamental but rarer in gardens is the Asian species *L. formosana*, which has pretty tri-lobed leaves and a narrow conical habit.

GROWING NOTES

Most of the liquidambars in cultivation are very adaptable to climates from warm to cool. They require full sun, which encourages good foliage colour, and an open aspect. The trees are very popular in streetscapes and urban designs, as they will tolerate pollution and infrequent watering; however, they are always best when growing without restrictions, and lopping ruins their shapely canopies. Note that the colours of the autumn leaves can vary from tree to tree, and even individuals can change tones slightly throughout the years.

LIRIODENDRON TULIPIFERA

TULIP TREE

A graceful giant, especially in autumn colours, the tulip tree is best in open garden spaces. The flower's form gives this genus its common name.

The tulip tree is one of the garden's legends. Imposingly large and capable of living for centuries, *Liriodendron tulipifera* is not a tree you plant on a whim: it is the sort of tree that makes a garden. George Washington knew it. The two tulip trees he planted in the mid-1850s on his family estate in Mount Vernon, Virginia, tower above that landscape today. Each more than 50 metres (150 ft) in height, they are probably the most famous of their kind.

Endemic to eastern North America, *L. tulipifera* is one of only two species in the genus *Liriodendron*. The other, *L. chinense*, is from China and less well known. Both are commonly called the tulip tree for their unusual cup-shaped flowers, although

The tulip tree will define the garden's character. Its leaves are botanically unusual, shaped by four lobes.

they are actually related to magnolias. The tulip trees also share a distinctive botanical quality: four-lobed leaves. *L. tulipifera* is the more commonly grown species, and has cultivars such as 'Aureomarginatum', with new leaves that have yellow edges, and 'Fastigiatum', which has a narrow, upright habit.

GROWING NOTES

Liriodendron tulipifera prefers cool, moist climates. The trees will grow in more temperate areas, but the spectacular colour of the autumn foliage may be compromised. They need full sun and deep, rich, well-drained soil. Water generously during spring and summer, and protect them from hot dry winds in warm climates. Tulip trees grow fairly quickly, but flowering, usually from spring to midsummer depending on the climate, will be infrequent until maturity. In cultivation, these trees generally reach about 30 metres (90 ft) in height and are suitable for large gardens only.

METASEQUOIA GLYPTOSTROBOIDES
DAWN REDWOOD

The dawn redwood is a rarity. A deciduous conifer, its foliage turns russet in autumn and the tree drops branchlets rather than single leaves.

The dawn redwood is a reminder of the preciousness of trees. Until fairly recently, this deciduous conifer (one of only a few conifers with this habit) was thought to be extinct and known only to humankind as a fossil. However, in the 1940s a single specimen of *Metasequoia glyptostroboides* was discovered growing in the gardens of a temple in China. Within a few years, cuttings and seeds of this tree were distributed globally, the species (the only one in the genus) was saved, and that dawn redwood's descendants are now seen throughout the world, in parks and gardens and even as bonsai—evoking a sense of wonder wherever they grow.

GROWING NOTES

Dawn redwoods thrive in cool to cold, moist climates where they grow rapidly to about 30 metres (120 ft) or more. The trees will also adapt to warmer regions, but may only reach about 15 metres (45 ft) in height. They grow in full sun or part shade, but require shelter from strong wind. Potted plants and specimens in warmer gardens should be well watered and protected from hot sun.

NYSSA SYLVATICA
TUPELO

The brilliant autumnal hues of tupelo leaves are elegantly displayed by the tree's shapely canopy of sweeping branches.

The brilliant autumn foliage of the tupelo transforms the tree into a towering inferno of colour. Its superb seasonal display is enhanced by a large conical canopy, broad at the base and tapering to an apex, of near-horizontal branches that give the tree a graceful, flared appearance. The genus, *Nyssa*, is suitably named after the water nymph of Greek mythology because tupelos flourish in water-rich soils. The most commonly grown species in gardens is *Nyssa sylvatica*, which is native to woodlands of North America where it grows impressively to 30 metres (120 ft) in height.

GROWING NOTES

Although *Nyssa sylvatica* will adapt to some temperate areas, it only develops its best deciduous colour when planted in full sun in cool to cold climates. Tupelos require deep moist soil, thriving in swampy conditions, and they resent transplanting. The trees should not be pruned; instead, their inherently graceful habits should be allowed to develop naturally.

PARROTIA PERSICA
PERSIAN IRONWOOD

The Persian ironwood has a seasonal presence without imposing size. The tree is versatile in designs, from small gardens to woodlands and streetscapes.

Also known as Persian witch hazel, this deciduous tree creates a dramatic impact in the garden with big bold leaves that are glossy green in spring and summer but in autumn become golden-yellow, orange and crimson. Originating around the Caspian Sea, the Caucasus and in northern Iran, *Parrotia persica* belongs to a genus of only one species. Although it can grow to 20 metres (60 ft) tall in its native habitats, in cultivation the Persian ironwood is usually 6–8 metres (18–24 ft) in height and may have shrub-like habits. The tree is dense with branches and foliage, forming a compact canopy. Persian ironwoods flower in late winter, often before the leaves appear. The blooms are tiny and without petals but abundantly cover the trees in a bright red haze.

GROWING NOTES

Persian ironwoods prefer cool, moist climates; although they grow well in warmer gardens, the foliage won't change colour in autumn. The trees are best in full sun, and deep, rich, well-drained soil. Water regularly throughout spring and summer.

PISTACIA CHINENSIS
PISTACHIO

This purely ornamental pistachio is cultivated not for nuts (these come from another species) but for its leaves, which display the most brilliant autumnal tones of flaming red, orange and gold. Originating from China and Japan, *Pistacia chinensis* can grow to 20 metres (60 ft) tall in its natural habitat, but in gardens it is usually half that height, and easy to place in designs. The canopy is rounded and broad, with compound leaves casting fluttery shade in spring and summer, and providing spectacular colour in autumn. Male and female flowers are produced on separate trees: the catkins (which are male flowers) are quite decorative and appear in spring; female flowers may be followed by berry-like fruits.

The pistachio's fine leaflets form an attractive canopy which becomes inflamed with colour in autumn; the tree suits many garden situations and designs.

GROWING NOTES

Pistachios are deciduous trees that grow in cool to warm climates, but their autumn foliage is better with colder winters. Full sun is best for growth and also for leaf colour. The soil should be well drained, preferably enriched with aged organic matter. Water regularly to establish the plants, after which they are tolerant of long dry periods.

PLATANUS SPECIES & HYBRIDS
PLANE TREE

The plane tree isn't the sort of tree you find in most gardens, but it is one that most gardeners know. Plane trees are fond and familiar features of cities, avenues and parks, characterised by massive size, mottled trunks and large, lobed leaves. Most commonly seen of these are the sycamores, *Platanus occidentalis*, from North America; the oriental planes, *P. orientalis*, from the Mediterranean and western Asia; and the London plane tree, a hybrid, *P.* x *acerifolia* (syn. *P.* x *hybrida*), which is extensively planted in European cities. All plane trees are deciduous, and will become very tall. They usually grow to 30–35 metres (90–115 ft) in height, with a similar spread, and the sycamore may tower to 50 metres (150 ft), placing it among the ornamental giants.

GROWING NOTES

Plane trees are extremely adaptable to climates from cold to subtropical. They are suitable only for large gardens, in open sunny aspects. The soil should be deep and well drained, but not necessarily rich. Avoid heavy-handed pruning of the canopy which spoils the tree's natural shape.

The plane tree is best in large garden spaces. The London plane tree (left) is a hybrid, and one of the most commonly planted types of these trees.

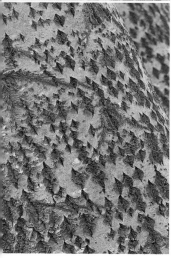

POPULUS SPECIES
POPLAR

The poplar's trademark is its tall and columnar habit—a distinct feature wherever the tree appears. Poplars have become classic trees of avenues, but are also familiar in the form of gigantic windbreaks and screens in rural landscapes. They are, however, usually unsuitable for many gardens: fast-growing, with an average height of about 30 metres (90 ft), poplars have very extensive root systems that are useful for stabilising soil but a nightmare near buildings. Some of the beautiful forms for large-scale designs include the aspen, *Populus tremula*, which has orange-red autumn leaves; the silver or white poplar, *P. alba*; the cottonwood, *P. deltoides*; and the famous spire-shaped *P. nigra* 'Italica', which is commonly known as the Lombardy poplar.

GROWING NOTES

Poplars adapt to most climates from cold to warm. They should be planted in full sun and deep soil that has a good water supply. Some species, such as the cottonwood, will tolerate coastal conditions as well as mild drought. All poplars are suitable only for very large gardens or rural settings.

The poplar's well-known types include the silver poplar (top and above) and the Lombardy poplar (right), which forms a tall narrow spire that turns golden in autumn.

QUERCUS SPECIES

OAK

The oak is more than a tree. It is a sacred arboreal being that stands longer than humankind and is part of our collective history. Oaks gave us timber when we started to build, food for stock, cork (that consequential bark), dyes and tannin, shelter and, some say, wisdom too. In gardens, oaks have also given us longevity—for the tree you plant today will be a feature for future generations.

There are about 600 species of oak tree, naturally ranging across the temperate parts of the northern hemisphere. One of the most symbolic is *Quercus robur*, commonly known as the English oak but actually endemic to Europe, northern Africa and western Asia as well. This species is the archetypal oak: deciduous, with gently lobed and rounded leaves, towering to 20 metres (60 ft) tall and wide, and capable of living for centuries—there are individuals in Europe that are reputed to be more than 500 years old.

Also reverential is the pin oak, *Q. palustris,* from eastern North America, which grows to 20 metres (60 ft) in height with a light, tapering canopy of sharply lobed, shiny leaves

Depending on the species, oaks may be deciduous or evergreen. However, many of the ornamental forms are deciduous and feature colourful autumn leaves.

that turn brilliant red in autumn. However, its seasonal colours are surpassed by the scarlet oak, *Q. coccinea*, which is endemic to the same area, slightly taller-growing, and regarded as one of the best oaks for autumn foliage displays.

GROWING NOTES

Depending on the origins of the species, there are oak trees for every climate except the tropics. They are suitable only for large gardens, where they can develop their impressive heights and canopies. Oaks are best in open aspects and full sun, and prefer deep, rich, well-drained soil. The fallen leaves of the deciduous types make a great mulch for the trees.

Oak trees are stately garden features, in formal or informal designs. The pin oak (opposite and above left) is distinguished by its tapering habit and sharply lobed leaves.

ROBINIA PSEUDOACACIA 'FRISIA'
GOLDEN ROBINIA

The elegant beauty of the golden robinia belies its tough constitution. This deciduous tree, originating from North America, is remarkably adaptable to designs, from street plantings to feature trees and small gardens. It grows fairly quickly, to about 10 metres (30 ft) in height, and forms a broad but airy canopy that develops a weeping appearance with age. All year round, the golden robinia has graceful features. In spring, the tree has pendent sprays of white, wisteria-like, perfumed flowers and its fern-like leaves are iridescent light green. Throughout summer, the canopy casts lacy shade, and in autumn, the foliage changes to bright buttery yellow.

GROWING NOTES

The golden robinia grows well in warm to cool climates, although it's not suitable for tropical areas. The plants need full sun for best foliage colour, and prefer deep, well-drained soil. The variety 'Frisia' is usually grafted onto rootstocks of the species (which is vigorous but not so desirable with spiny and suckering habits). Once established, do not disturb the roots of grafted golden robinias, as this encourages suckers.

Golden robinias are graceful feature trees in all seasons but they are also very versatile in designs.

SALIX SPECIES
WILLOW

Willows have an affinity with watery settings, but some forms, such as the pussy willow (below), can be planted as screens or feature trees.

The willows may be easily recognised among trees, with their distinctive leaf-and-wand habits, yet they are not a frequent sight in gardens. Instead, the willows' realms are parks and landscapes, which can accommodate their gigantic root systems. All of the 400 or so species of *Salix* originate in the northern hemisphere, and some of the best known include the weeping willow, *Salix babylonica*, which grows to 15 metres (45 ft) high and wide; the smaller-growing goat willow or pussy willow, *S. caprea*, with silky catkins; the Chilean willow, *S. chilensis*, which has a narrow habit that suits windbreaks; and the corkscrew or tortured willow, *S. matsudana* 'Tortuosa', with twisted stems that are favoured for indoor decoration.

GROWING NOTES
Willow trees are very adaptable to climates from subtropical to cold. They are best in full sun, and will grow in any soil that has plenty of moisture. While these trees love a watery setting next to streams or ponds, where they can help to prevent erosion by stabilising the soil, willows dislike swampy conditions that are permanently wet.

SAPIUM SEBIFERUM
CHINESE TALLOW TREE

Originating in the warm woodlands of southern China and Japan, the Chinese tallow tree is a very dependable ornamental and is grown in many parts of the world. It is a feature of streetscapes, parks and gardens, and rarely exceeds 12 metres (36 ft) in height, but can also be pruned without ruining its broad and shapely canopy, and so may be grown in courtyards and other restricted spaces. It is also one of the few deciduous trees to have great autumn foliage in warm climates, and will even colour well in subtropical regions.

GROWING NOTES
The Chinese tallow tree is very adaptable to climates from cool to subtropical, although an open sunny aspect produces best foliage colour. The plants prefer enriched and well-drained soils but aren't fussy. They need regular watering for the first few years after planting; once established, these trees are very resistant to drought. Note that like all members of the euphorbia family to which it belongs, the Chinese tallow tree has a milky sap that can cause skin irritations.

The Chinese tallow tree is very easy to grow; the foliage is bright green in spring and summer, but colours orange, purple and red in autumn.

ULMUS SPECIES & CULTIVARS
ELM

L ong considered to be among the most desirable of garden trees, the noble elms have taken a battering in the last century. This hiccup in the history of the elm is all because of a beetle which carries a fungus, which causes a disease that kills the trees. Although it has been known since about 1910, the Dutch elm disease didn't reach epidemic proportions until the 1960s, when it promptly wiped out many species of *Ulmus* in Europe and North America and, with them, some of the world's oldest elm trees.

However, thanks to the efforts of modern research, which has identified methods of control as well as certain species and hybrids that appear resistant to Dutch elm disease, and to dedicated gardeners who fearlessly re-planted, the elms are on the rise again.

Ever-popular is the wych or Scotch elm, *Ulmus glabra*, a non-suckering species that can grow to 35 metres (105 ft) in height;

The golden elm (left) is valued for its colourful foliage, but the tree also has blossoms of a rare pale green that appear before the leaves in spring.

Elms are renowned for impressive canopies. 'Pendula' (right) is a weeping form of *Ulmus glabra*. The Chinese elm (below) is also known as the lacebark elm, for the trunk's beauty.

especially its cultivar 'Lutescens', the golden elm, which only grows to about 15 metres (45 ft) and has a rounded canopy of pale yellow-green leaves that are richly coloured in autumn. Also favoured is the Chinese elm, *U. parvifolia*, a vigorous species that grows 15–20 metres (45–60 ft) tall and wide. Deciduous or semi-deciduous depending on the climate, this elm has small leaves in an elegantly spreading canopy and beautiful bark which adds to its charms.

GROWING NOTES

Elm trees are best in cool moist climates but many, such as the Scotch and the Chinese elms, will adapt to warmer gardens. They require full sun and open aspects where their canopies can spread. The soil should be moist and well drained, and the plants need ample watering in spring and summer.

fruit
trees

These days, many gardeners cultivate fruit trees just for pleasure—whether to eat or to look at. The fruiting displays of trees and shrubs are seasonal highlights, as much as their flowers or leaves. Trees and shrubs that bear fruits, pods and berries bring an added decorative element to the garden, but also an air of abundance. Fruit-laden plants make the garden feel rich.

Fruiting trees and shrubs provide edible crops in gardens but can also create decorative displays that last for months. This page: A stand of peach trees is a garden in itself. Previous pages: The redcurrant, *Ribes rubrum*.

This chapter includes trees and shrubs that are grown for edible fruit, and also those for ornamental purposes (not all are consumable). While some plants require specific conditions to produce good results, many are adaptable and can even be grown in pots. In nature, most plants that flower also bear fruit—so any garden can enjoy the visual delights of fruiting shrubs and trees.

There are fruit trees and shrubs to suit any garden and climate, including many that can be grown in containers. Left: A grapefruit as a feature tree. Right: Crabapples. Following pages: A plum tree is ornamental in all seasons.

ARBUTUS UNEDO
STRAWBERRY TREE

This ancient tree—a survivor of the ice ages—is only found naturally in the Mediterranean region, in the north west of the United States, and around Killarney, Ireland. The common name refers to the strawberry-like appearance of the fruits. It has been suggested that the Latin species name, *unedo* ('I eat one'), refers to the fruit's taste—so unpalatable that those who have eaten one would not eat two. Ornamentally, however, the fruits of *Arbutus unedo* are hard to surpass. The clusters can take a year to ripen red on the evergreen tree and so appear in conjunction with the flowers on a background of dark leathery leaves—a delicious-looking display, even if it isn't.

Evergreen and compact, the strawberry tree suits small garden spaces. In autumn and winter, flowers appear and the previous year's fruits turn red.

GROWING NOTES

The strawberry tree's diverse origins allow it to adapt to various climates. It grows in warm to cool areas, and will tolerate frost and wind as well as mild coastal conditions. The plants prefer full sun and well-drained soil. The Irish strawberry tree is the most commonly grown variety: it grows 5–8 metres (15–24 ft) in height and has a dense habit with a broad leafy crown.

ARDISIA CRENATA
CORALBERRY

The coralberry is a small and compact shrub but it has a bold display of berries, and for several months of the year it is festooned with opulent clusters of ornamental fruits that look like perfect plastic cherries. These are offset by evergreen leaves, large, wavy-edged and leathery, arranged in whorl-like formations. The coralberry, having warm and tropical origins in forest understoreys, thrives in shady gardens but can also be grown in containers and indoors. The shrub only grows about 1 metre (3 ft) tall; usually potted plants have a single stem, while those in the garden normally develop multi-stemmed habits.

GROWING NOTES

Ardisia crenata (syn. *A. crispa*), the most commonly grown species of coralberry, prefers tropical to temperate climates but also tolerates light frost in cooler gardens. It requires shade or partly shaded positions, such as under evergreen trees, where it is protected from strong wind and sun, and prefers organically rich, well-drained soil. Indoors, the plant does best in well-lit areas such as close to sunny windows.

The gleaming fruits of coralberry remain on the plant for several months, starkly contrasted against the dark leathery leaves.

CARYA ILLINOINENSIS
PECAN

The pecan, also known as hickory, originates from the southern United States but the trees are commercially cultivated in many parts of the world. Adaptable to a range of climates and fairly fast-growing, to about 10–15 metres (30–45 ft) in height and 8 metres (25 ft) wide, the pecan is also valuable in gardens: it has a classically shaped canopy of compound leaves that colour yellow and orange in autumn, and masses of catkins in spring. There are self-pollinating types, too, which means that one tree can beget a pecan crop; however, a few cross-pollinating varieties will not only produce greater harvests but also create an attractive stand.

Apart from their crops, pecans are also highly ornamental garden trees with colourful leaves in autumn and catkins in spring.

GROWING NOTES

Pecans adapt to many climates but prefer areas with cool, moist winters and warm summers. They dislike extremes of hot or cold. The trees require open sunny positions and well-drained, organically enriched soil for best performance. Do not prune once established as the catkins (hence nuts) are borne on the ends of branches. Grafted trees bear crops after about five years but seedlings can take twice as long.

CERATONIA SILIQUA
CAROB

Long before it became famous as a chocolate substitute, carob was an influential crop. In Turkey and the eastern Mediterranean regions where it originates, carob is used as a nutritious stock fodder, and the seeds, which are extremely hard, reputedly founded the carat weight by which jewellers measure gems. In gardens, *Ceratonia siliqua* is an attractive and useful evergreen: it can grow to 10 metres (30 ft) in height, and has a broad canopy, up to 8 metres (24 ft) wide, with shiny compound leaves that cast a lovely dappled shade. Carobs are adaptable, too, and once established these trees are very tough and will resist strong wind and drought.

The seed pods of carob ripen from pale green to shiny dark brown; the tree is also grown in gardens for its evergreen and shade-casting canopy.

GROWING NOTES
Carob trees grow in climates from subtropical to mildly cool, and will tolerate light frost. The plants prefer full sun, and the soil should be well drained but not necessarily rich. Like most members of the legume family, carobs don't usually require fertilising. For good crops, plant several trees and ensure there are both male and female flowers.

COCOS NUCIFERA
COCONUT PALM

The coconut palm is such an extraordinary plant—almost all parts of it, from fruit to fibre, are useful and commercial—that we sometimes forget to admire its beauty. As an ornamental, the coconut is tall-growing, to about 20 metres (60 ft) or more in ideal conditions. It has a singular trunk that is slightly curved and topped by giant arching fronds in a tall feathery canopy. On its own, or planted in close-knit groves, or in stately rows, the coconut palm evokes a distinctly tropical and verdant atmosphere in the garden. In tropical climates, coconut palms bear fruit at 4–5 years but most plants don't produce steady crops until aged about ten.

GROWING NOTES

Coconut palms grow in warm and subtropical climates but are best, and will only set fruit, in the tropics. They do well in glasshouses in cooler areas. The plants are extremely tolerant of exposed coastal conditions. They prefer full sun, but appreciate some shade when young. The soil must be very well drained, but not necessarily rich.

The arching fronds of the coconut palm form an exotic canopy; the plants only produce fruit in the tropics.

COTONEASTER SPECIES & CULTIVARS

Cotoneasters have many garden uses and their decorative clusters of autumn and winter berries are long-lasting.

The cotoneasters are a well-known group of shrubs with a reputation for being easy to grow, adaptable to a range of garden conditions, and versatile in designs. Most have bright red, ornamental berries, their main visual attraction, though their spring flowers can be quite pretty and some also have brilliant autumn leaves. Among the popular types for gardens are *Cotoneaster horizontalis* and its cultivars, which are semi-deciduous with low spreading branches, intricately interwoven and ideal for trailing over walls and banks, and the evergreens, such as *C. lacteus*, which are favoured for hedges.

GROWING NOTES

Cotoneasters grow in most garden climates; however, they do prefer cool areas and are unsuitable for the tropics. The plants are best in full sun, which encourages dense growth. They aren't fussy but will appreciate a soil that is enriched with organic matter. Once established, cotoneasters are tolerant of dry periods but they grow better with regular watering. Note that birds love the berries and can spread the seeds.

CYDONIA OBLONGA
QUINCE

Native to the Middle East but long naturalised in the Mediterranean region, the quince has been cultivated since ancient times. To the Classical Greeks and Romans, the fruit was a symbol of love, happiness and fertility, while medieval gardeners enjoyed the quince in jams, pies and jellies. These days, quince trees are still valued in the garden for their fruits, but also for their spring displays of pale pink blossoms that precede the crop, and for their rounded canopies of deciduous leaves which turn golden in autumn.

The fruit of quinces are formed in summer and ripen in mid-autumn to bright yellow; they are edible, decorative and fragrant, too.

GROWING NOTES

Quinces will grow in climates from cool to subtropical. They are best in full sun and moist, well-drained soil. The trees are fairly slow-growing, eventually reaching about 6 metres (18 ft) in height. Cultivars of quince that are favoured in gardens are self-pollinating, so only one tree is required, and some will bear fruit after only three or four years. If necessary, prune the trees in winter while they are dormant. Handle the fruits with care as they can bruise easily.

CYPHOMANDRA BETACEA
TAMARILLO

The tamarillo is also known as the tree tomato, but it's actually more closely related to the aubergine. Originating from South America, the tamarillo is an evergreen shrub or small tree, growing to 3–4 metres (9–12 ft) in height, with a vase-shaped habit and a lightly branched canopy. While the smooth-skinned, egg-shaped fruits are edible, cooked or raw, they are also decorative on the tree. The tamarillo's fruits are large, about 7 cm (3 inches) long, usually bright red but alternatively yellow, and hang off the tree's branches like clusters of baubles. With each taking many months to mature fully, from summer throughout autumn to winter, the fruits create a long-lasting display.

The fruits of the tamarillo hang among its large, heart-shaped leaves, creating a colourful display for many months while they ripen.

GROWING NOTES

Tamarillos prefer warm to tropical climates, and they are intolerant of frost. The plants are best in full sun and soil that is well drained and enriched with organic matter. They require protection from strong wind, and regular watering in dry seasons. Tamarillos can also be grown in containers. These trees may be short-lived, even in ideal conditions, but can be propagated from seed in spring.

DIOSPYROS KAKI
PERSIMMON

For many centuries the persimmon has been grown for its vitamin-rich fruit—the species originates in China and has also been cultivated in Japan since about 800 CE—but in gardens its foliage and form are valued as well. Persimmons are deciduous trees that can grow to 10 metres (30 ft) in height, although fruiting cultivars are usually smaller, and they have spreading, umbrella-shaped canopies of glossy ovate leaves which turn brilliant orange, red and burgundy in autumn. The colourful foliage often coincides with the ripening of the rounded fruit, creating a sumptuous seasonal display.

Persimmon fruits ripen from late summer to mid-autumn, depending on the variety. The trees are ideal for small gardens.

GROWING NOTES
Persimmons prefer cool to mild climates and moist environments. The plants are best in full sun and enriched, well-drained soils. They need regular watering, especially while in full growth during spring and summer. Most persimmons grown in gardens are cultivars, with many being grafted because seedlings can be unreliable.

ELAEOCARPUS RETICULATUS
BLUEBERRY ASH

The blueberry ash is one of Australia's distinctive ornamental trees. Originating from eastern parts of that country, in a range of habitats and climates, this evergreen has an elegantly shaped canopy of dark green leathery leaves that are reddish-pink when new. In the wild, the tree can grow to 15 metres (45 ft) in height, but in cultivation it is usually a tidy 8–10 metres (25–30 ft) tall. The crown rarely spreads more than 5 metres (15 ft) and tapers with age. Sprays of flowers are produced in spring and summer. Bell-shaped and fringed, these are white in the species but there are also pink-flowered forms. The flowers are followed in autumn by hard, shiny, ornamental berries that ripen to a distinctive deep blue.

The blueberry ash is an elegant evergreen with bell-shaped fringed flowers followed by decorative blue berries.

GROWING NOTES

The blueberry ash is very adaptable in climates from warm and tropical to cool with freezing winter temperatures. It tolerates full sun, but is best in sheltered part shade. The soil should be well drained and fairly rich. It is an ideal feature tree and can also be grown in large containers.

FICUS CARICA
FIG TREE

The fig tree has been cultivated for thousands of years and was grown by ancient civilisations such as the Egyptians, the Romans and the Greeks. It belongs to the great genus, *Ficus* (see page 303), although the origin of *Ficus carica* is somewhat obscure: some experts say it came from the Middle East, others claim western Asia, while most people associate it with the Mediterranean region. Figs have long been grown in gardens worldwide; and there are many cultivars. Good fig trees can produce fruit after a few years and, once matured, the best ones will bear crops twice each year.

The fruit of fig trees appears in summer or autumn; the flowers are formed inside the fruits.

GROWING NOTES
Fig trees are very adaptable, but they do require a fairly long and cool winter to set fruit. They are tolerant of frost and low temperatures, but dislike hot, humid summer weather. Fig trees are deciduous, with dense foliage, and will grow to about 8 metres (24 ft) tall, although old trees can reach much greater heights. Only one tree is required for fruit to be produced. Beware of birds and fruit fly: they like figs, too.

ILEX SPECIES & CULTIVARS
HOLLY

The hedging of holly is an ancient practice that takes advantage of its impenetrably dense and evergreen foliage. These plants are very long-lived and hardy.

Holly is a plant that history has made significant. In ancient times, it was used to ward off evil spirits; it was also sacred to pre-Christian deities before it became associated with Christianity and particularly the season of Christmas. Now, in the modern world, its spiny leaves together with clusters of decorative red berries are recognised everywhere—holly has seeped into our psyche.

The holly of legends is the common holly, *Ilex aquifolium*, which originates in Europe and Asia. It naturally grows into a small evergreen tree, about 10 metres (30 ft) in height, and makes a lovely feature. However, common holly is also often used in hedges or topiary. Even hundreds of years ago, there were cultivars of common holly, and there are many available today: some have variegated leaves or yellow berries; others are self-fertile; and there's the hedgehog types which have spines all over their leaves and no fruit.

The common holly has white flowers followed by red berries in autumn and winter. Some cultivars have been grown for centuries, including those with variegated leaves edged in gold, silver or cream.

Also popular in gardens are smaller-growing, shrub-like hollies such as *I. cornuta*, the Chinese or horned holly, which has larger leaves and berries and so is often preferred for decoration, and *I. crenata*, the Japanese or box-leaved holly, with more diminutive leaves and small black berries. Both species also have many cultivars.

GROWING NOTES

Hollies generally prefer cool to cold climates, but also adapt to warmer areas; the Chinese holly is the most suitable for warm gardens. The hollies will tolerate frost, strong winds, pollution and drought once established. The plants are best in full sun and rich well-drained soil. Most holly plants are either male or female, and only females produce berries (except in certain cultivars). Holly can be trimmed to shape throughout the year, and, if necessary, pruned more heavily in winter; when handling, wear protective gloves and clothing.

MACADAMIA SPECIES & CULTIVARS
MACADAMIA

The lush, evergreen canopy of the mature macadamia tree casts dense cool shade in the warm garden.

These magnificent trees are native to the east coast of Australia, but their species and cultivars are grown in warm climates in many parts of the world and they are extensively farmed in Hawaii. Commercially valued for their succulent nuts, macadamias also make imposing feature trees in gardens. Evergreens with broad, rounded canopies, they can grow to 20 metres (60 ft) in height in ideal conditions, although in cultivation they are usually half as tall. The foliage is dark, shiny and slightly leathery, with new growth that is often tinged red, and sprays of pink and white flowers in spring. The nuts mature in late summer to autumn, and, when ripe, they fall from the tree.

GROWING NOTES

Macadamia trees require warm to tropical climates and are intolerant of frost. They prefer full sun, in an open position, and deep, well-drained soil that has been enriched with aged organic matter before planting. Water young plants generously in spring and summer, but be aware that the trees can be susceptible to root rot.

MALUS X DOMESTICA
APPLE

From the Ballerina and Pink Lady to Delicious, Willie Sharp, Granny Smith and Gravenstein, apples are among the most popular trees in the world. *Malus* x *domestica*, the apple, is a derivative of the crab apple (see page 234), an improvement that has been exploited for more than 3,000 years.

Today, there more than 2,000 registered apple varieties, and many have been specifically created for home gardening. While cultivated apples are best as grafted or budded trees, the modern garden types (often trademarked varieties) are also more adaptable to a range of conditions, less prone to pests and diseases, and fruit more reliably—addressing the problems that were previously the apple's downfall. The Ballerina-types are especially popular, as these are small and upright, with central fruiting stems that don't require much pruning; some can even be grown in pots. Re-makes of heritage varieties are favoured, too, whether trained in traditional espaliers and fans, or allowed to develop into full-blown orchard-style beauties.

Even if they didn't produce popular fruits, apples would be among the garden's most beautiful trees: blossoms of Granny Smith (above); apple tree trained as a cordon (right).

GROWING NOTES

Most apple cultivars are best in cool to temperate climates, although some are tolerant of frost and others adapt to warm gardens. They must have full sun and protection from strong wind. Apple trees require deep, rich, well-drained soil, and should be regularly watered during the growing season. More than one tree is required to produce reliable crops, and the best fruits are usually obtained when different cultivars are grown. Choose varieties that flower at the same time, and plant them in a grove.

Unless considering a modern trademark type, it's worthwhile seeking a specialist nursery in your local region—your garden's climatic conditions are the ruling factors when selecting apple varieties, and a reputable source will also give you valuable advice on pruning, care and planting.

Apple trees are deciduous, with autumn foliage that changes colour as the harvest ripens. Popular cultivars include the Jonathan (above left) and Granny Smith (above).

MORUS SPECIES & CULTIVARS
MULBERRY

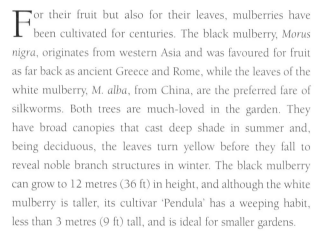

Most mulberries will eventually grow into grand trees, but there are also smaller cultivars that can be neatly trained as weeping standards.

For their fruit but also for their leaves, mulberries have been cultivated for centuries. The black mulberry, *Morus nigra*, originates from western Asia and was favoured for fruit as far back as ancient Greece and Rome, while the leaves of the white mulberry, *M. alba*, from China, are the preferred fare of silkworms. Both trees are much-loved in the garden. They have broad canopies that cast deep shade in summer and, being deciduous, the leaves turn yellow before they fall to reveal noble branch structures in winter. The black mulberry can grow to 12 metres (36 ft) in height, and although the white mulberry is taller, its cultivar 'Pendula' has a weeping habit, less than 3 metres (9 ft) tall, and is ideal for smaller gardens.

GROWING NOTES

Mulberries grow in climates from cool to subtropical. They like full sun, and adapt to most soils, but shouldn't be planted in exposed situations. Only one plant is required to produce fruit. Be aware that the big old trees can bear great crops which then get messy underfoot, and the berries can stain. Birds love mulberries, too, and are infamous for spreading seeds.

OLEA EUROPAEA
OLIVE TREE

For as long as there have been gardeners, there have been olives. These trees were cultivated thousands of years ago, and some individual plants have been around for centuries. Not surprisingly, *Olea europaea*, the common olive, which originates in the Mediterranean region, has numerous cultivars: many are grown for fruit, others for oil, while some are versatile garden varieties. Evergreen and generally growing 8–12 metres (24–36 ft) in height, olives make great specimen trees. They may also be clipped into hedges or grown in pots. The tree's leaves, apart from their fame as peace offerings (a tradition dating back to Roman times), are features, too—dark green with grey undersides, the foliage shimmers silver when brushed by a breeze.

GROWING NOTES

Olive trees are very adaptable to climates from cool to warm; they also endure coastal conditions, and drought and frost once established. They require full sun and well-drained soil. Only one tree is required to produce fruits, however, seedling-grown plants can take many years to do so—grafted trees are quicker to mature.

Apart from their valuable crops, olive trees can be used in various designs, including hedging. Flowers in spring and summer are followed by fruits in late summer and autumn.

The Chinese lantern plant has a distinct and decorative calyx which is filled with air and encloses the fruit that is a single scarlet berry.

PHYSALIS ALKEKENGI
CHINESE LANTERN

Although the fruits of the Chinese lantern, *Physalis alkekengi*, are edible, the plant is more frequently appreciated by gardeners for its ornamental calyces (the outer covering that encloses the berry), which are papery and translucent and look very much like lanterns alight. Related to the cape gooseberry (*P. peruviana*) and part of the potato family, the Chinese lantern plant is a multi-stemmed shrub or perennial which rarely exceeds 1 metre (3 ft) in height. For most of the year, the plants are rather uninteresting, but in autumn, when hung with their bright lanterns, they come to life. Popular cultivars of the species include 'Gigantea', which has larger-than-normal calyces, and 'Pygmaea', a dwarf form.

GROWING NOTES

The Chinese lantern will grow in most garden climates from cool to near tropical, but dislikes arid areas. The plants require full sun or part shade, with protection from strong wind. They prefer enriched, well-drained soil, and may be grown in pots. The fruiting stems can be cut for indoor arrangements, and the calyces retain their colour when dried.

PRUNUS SPECIES & CULTIVARS
STONE FRUITS

Stone fruit trees provide welcome crops but also great garden beauty. The Hale (above and right) is a popular cultivar of the peach tree.

When Arcadian orchards come to mind, so do the stone fruits—such as the plum, peach, apricot and cherry. These members of the genus *Prunus* are elite in the world of fruit trees. Some have been cultivated for thousands of years— the plum in Asia, the peach in China, the cherry and the almond around the Mediterranean. For many gardeners (as well as for artists and poets), then and now, they are the ultimate in trees—with spring blossoms, followed by sumptuous harvests, colourful autumn foliage and bare-branched winter beauty.

The stone fruits are an extensive group, within a most influential clan (see also pages 176 and 246–9), which includes the plum, greengage and damson (all are *Prunus domestica*);

Prunus trees are appealing in all seasons, whether they are bare branched or in bloom, fruit or leaf: the sweet cherry, *Prunus avium* (opposite and below); plum tree, *P. domestica*, in flower (left).

the peach (*P. persica*) and its variety the nectarine; the apricot (*P. armeniaca*), and the cherries (*P. avium* and *P. cerasus*). There are, of course, innumerable cultivars, and many have been created specifically for gardeners' needs. You'll find forms that are self-fertile, or ideal for training into standards, cordons and espaliers. Others are grafted to improve their performance or so that they bear good crops as young trees. In choosing *Prunus* for fruiting purposes, it's worthwhile seeking a reputable supplier to ensure a quality tree for your garden.

GROWING NOTES

The diverse origins of stone fruits allow gardeners in most climates to enjoy them, in one form or another. Most prefer cool climates, although the peach (and hence the nectarine) adapt to warmer gardens too. Plums, on the other hand, require a long period of winter chilling to set fruit. All are best in full sun and enriched, well-drained soil, with regular watering during the growing season.

There are many cultivars of pomegranates including low-growing forms that are ideal for containers, as well as varieties grown for their flowers.

PUNICA GRANATUM
POMEGRANATE

With the pomegranate, even the smallest garden can enjoy the pleasures of a fruiting tree. These deciduous trees or shrubs are easy to grow and will thrive in pots, on balconies, and in courtyards and other enclosed garden spaces. Pomegranates are ornamental in every way: they have dense rounded canopies of small shiny leaves which turn golden-yellow in autumn; flashy scarlet flowers in spring and summer; followed by glossy rounded red fruits—the pomegranate's prize. The fruits ripen best in climates with hot summers, but there are also cultivars grown for their flowers, which may be white, apricot or crimson, and some have double blooms.

GROWING NOTES

Pomegranates grow in most climates, but the fruiting types are best in areas with hot, dry summers and cool, wet winters; they are unsuitable for the tropics. The plants must have full sun and prefer well-drained soils enriched with organic matter. Once established, pomegranates are very tolerant of drought, however, regular watering in spring and summer promotes a better crop. Pruning is not required, but a light trim in late winter keeps the plants growing densely.

Decorative firethorn berries feature on the plant for months throughout autumn and winter; once the berries are coloured, the stems can be cut for indoor arrangements.

PYRACANTHA SPECIES
FIRETHORN

Most frequently seen in gardens as a formidable hedging plant—being tall, robust and evergreen with thorny branches—the firethorn's great ornamental feature is its decorative berries. Shiny and coloured red or orange depending on the species or cultivar, these are borne prolifically in clusters that last for months throughout autumn and winter. Birds love them, but unfortunately they can also spread the seeds and lead the plants astray; in some climates, firethorn can then become a weed. Fairly fast-growing, these shrubs can reach about 3–5 metres (9–15 ft) in height, and they make dramatic screens, hedges or espaliers.

GROWING NOTES

Firethorns grow in most climates, except the tropics; however, they do prefer cool, moist areas. The plants are best in full sun and well-drained soil, but will withstand strong wind and poor soils. Once established, they are also quite tolerant of dry periods. Free-form plants rarely need pruning; those to be trained can be trimmed and shaped at any time.

PYRUS SPECIES & CULTIVARS
PEAR

Whether grown for fruit or flower or even for leaf, pear trees are ornamental assets in the garden. The pear has it all—fine structure, graceful canopy, leaves with lovely autumnal tones, dainty white blossoms in spring and, of course, fruit, for which they have been cultivated for thousands of years. The ancient Greeks thought the pear godly, and the Romans were devoted to it. And throughout history, the pear has been immortalised in art, poetry and prose.

Today, there are thousands of pear varieties, with most being grown for fruit. Commonly, pear trees are grafted, to keep them manageable in size and more productive. Some cultivars of the fruiting type (*Pyrus communis*) go back hundreds of years, and are just as popular now, including 'Jargonelle', from the 1600s, and the self-fertile 'Conference', of the late 18th century.

Gardeners, however, are just as likely to appreciate the pear tree for its beauty, and some species are grown for flowers and leaves. The Manchurian pear (*P. ussuriensis*) and the Chinese or callery pear (*P. calleryana*) have outstanding blossom displays and rich autumn foliage colours. The weeping pear (*P. salicifolia*) is grown for its canopy of delicate, silvery-green leaves.

Most pear varieties are grown for fruit, such as 'Conference' (left), which has been popular for more than 200 years; however, some, like the weeping pear (above), are valued for their beauty.

In spring, the pear's blossoms cover the tree; one of their many charms. The Manchurian pear (below and opposite) is grown ornamentally, for flowers as well as for richly coloured autumn leaves.

GROWING NOTES

All pear trees are deciduous. The fruiting types prefer cool or temperate climates and are at their best when grown in Mediterranean-style conditions. The ornamental pears are more adaptable to warmer gardens, and will also tolerate coastal aspects, pollution and drought once established. All pear trees require full sun and well-drained soil that is preferably enriched. Where crops are concerned, obtain the plants from local specialist growers who can advise you on cultivars (some pears have specific pollination preferences), as well as care and maintenance.

RIBES SPECIES & CULTIVARS
CURRANTS

E ven though there are about 150 species of currants in the genus *Ribes*, only a few are common in gardens. For fruit, there's the blackcurrant (*Ribes nigrum*), the red or white currants (both *R. rubrum*) and the gooseberry (*R. uva-crispa*), and all these species have many cultivars as well. However, there is also the flowering currant, *R. sanguineum*, from North America, which is not so much grown for fruits (these are blue-black) as for its other decorative features: a graceful arching habit to about 2 metres (6 ft) in height, with pendent sprays of crimson, pink or white flowers in late spring.

Currant bushes bear delicious fruit and are also decorative; they include gooseberries (left) and blackcurrants (above).

GROWING NOTES
Most of the currants in cultivation require cool, moist climates. They prefer rich, well-drained soil and full sun, but will take light shade. Many of the plants naturally form dense bushes; however, the fruiting forms are usually routinely pruned to encourage good crops. Red and white currants may also be trained as cordons, standards or espaliers—very elegant features, especially when dripping with fruit.

VACCINIUM SPECIES & CULTIVARS
BLUEBERRY

In the right conditions, blueberry shrubs are fast-growing and can be long-lived. The fruits should be picked after they have ripened.

The blueberry isn't just delicious, it's ornamental too. These deciduous shrubs have bushy habits of bright green leaves that turn fiery red in autumn, and spring or summer clusters of bell-shaped flowers which are tiny and white, but may also be tinged pink. Then, of course, there are the berries, providing a brilliant display as they ripen, from late summer to autumn, depending on the plant type. In gardens (and commercial realms), blueberry plants are usually cultivars, with most deriving from the North American species *Vaccinium corymbosum*. There are many types available—generally known as lowbush, highbush or rabbit-eye—but for the best results, choose plants that suit your garden's climate.

GROWING NOTES

Blueberries prefer cool climates, where the plants can get sufficiently long chilling periods in winter; however, there are also hybrids for warmer gardens. All insist on acidic soil and regular watering. Some types may be grown in pots, which also ensures the conditions are lime-free. Cover fruiting plants with netting to protect the crop from birds.

CITRUS SPECIES & CULTIVARS

citrus

The influence of citrus trees is immeasurable. It's impossible to imagine human life without the orange, lemon, lime and their kin. In the garden, they are the most commonly planted of the fruit trees, featuring in pots, groves and orangeries, and giving gardeners all over the world the pleasure of growing fruit at home.

Citrus trees are ornamental

in the garden, as well as

productive. Clockwise from

top left: citrus blossoms;

Valencia orange; grapefruit

tree; and mandarin.

The citrus family's path to fame and fortune goes back at least 3,000 years. Most of the *Citrus* species hail from Asia, although their exact origins are blurred by cultivation throughout the millennia. And also, along the way, the ancestral species including the lemon, the lime, the oranges and the mandarin have evolved, producing many cultivars and hybrids, such as the grapefruit, the tangelo and the calamondin, to further extend their influence. *Citrus* is not just an important plant genus, it's a far-reaching dynasty.

The orange is a senior member of the citrus clan, having been cultivated for thousands of years. The Seville, *Citrus aurantium*, also known as the sour orange, was one of the first citrus to reach Europe, via the Crusaders and Spain, and this tree is often grown for its ornamental beauty as well as for its fruit, the purist's choice for marmalade.

Modern palettes, however, tend to prefer the sweet orange, *Citrus sinensis*, and its many varieties, including the Navels (of which there are several types) and the Valencias. The blood orange, another form of *C. sinensis*, is an old favourite of the Mediterranean region, but, with its red-coloured flesh and rind, has also found a niche with citrus connoisseurs and in cutting-edge cuisine.

Although lemons (*Citrus limon*) arrived in cultivation history much later than the oranges, they are now the most popular of citrus trees for home gardens. Lemon trees are very adaptable,

Citrus trees can be planted in many garden designs, from groves and avenues to features. Some, like the Meyer lemon, are prolific even as young trees and will also grow in pots.

and they are more tolerant of frost than many other citrus. Well-known forms include the Eureka, which is almost spineless and can produce fruit year round, and the Meyer, which is suitable for colder climates.

Mandarins (*Citrus reticulata*), or tangerines as they are sometimes known, are also popular for their ease of cultivation. All the mandarin cultivars will endure light frost, and they rarely exceed 3 metres (9 ft) in height, with foliage almost to the ground, which makes the fruit easy to harvest.

Other members of the citrus family which are frequently featured in gardens include the lime (*Citrus aurantiifolia*), a tropical delight, with its distinctive green fruit; the grapefruit (*C.* x *paradisi*), which is the offspring of the orange and the pomelo (*C. maxima*) and is believed to have originated from the West Indies; and the calamondin (x *Citrofortunella mitis*), a hybrid of the mandarin and the kumquat (which is related to *Citrus* but from the genus *Fortunella*).

The diversity of the citrus family ensures its suitability to a range of gardens. Many, such as the Seville orange, the mandarin and the grapefruit, make great feature trees. Others, like the Meyer lemon, the lime and the calamondin, can be easily grown in pots—on balconies, in courtyards and conservatories, or simply near the kitchen door.

Citrus are very rewarding trees for home gardens. Clockwise from top left: Tahitian limes; Navel oranges; grapefruits; and mandarins.

GROWING NOTES

Most forms of citrus prefer cool to warm climates; however, some will tolerate occasional light frost. Limes require tropical conditions, although the Tahitian type will grow in cooler gardens; grapefruits, too, are best in warmer regions. In cold climates, citrus are traditionally grown in large containers, so that they can be moved indoors when frost hits.

All citrus require full sun and shelter from strong winds. The soil should be very well drained and preferably enriched with aged organic matter. Water regularly and deeply, especially during the warmer months, and while the trees are in flower or fruit—this encourages a prolific and juicy crop. Feeding the trees, usually in late winter and at midsummer, will also reward at harvest time. Trim the trees only if necessary for shaping, because fruits are produced on mature wood. Most of the citrus types in garden cultivation are self-pollinating, which means that only one tree is required to produce fruit.

Importantly, gardeners should obtain citrus trees from a reputable supplier: the good plants are grafted, virus-free and resistant to root rot.

Citrus trees, like the mandarin (right), are evergreen and decorative year round, with glossy aromatic leaves in dense canopies, fragrant blossoms, as well as fruit.

PRUNING NOTES

The pruning of trees is a great skill, and sometimes will require the services of professionals. Here are a few tips for gardeners.

GENERAL PRUNING

For naturally beautiful trees and shrubs, limit your pruning—it's best to start with plants that suit your garden and purpose. Always use sharp, clean tools and create as little damage as possible.

Avoid pruning the canopies, except to remove weak or wayward growths, such as those that cross over other branches or clutter the tree's centre. Low branches can be removed to lift a tree's crown or develop vase-like shapes, but don't remove too many at once. Some young trees are best left to develop unpruned.

Deciduous plants are most easily pruned while their branches are bare and their structures are visible. However, with spring-flowering types, gardeners may prefer to wait until the blooms appear, so that branches can be cut for indoor decoration, or prune directly after the flowers are finished. Evergreen trees and shrubs can be pruned at any time, although preferably not during the growing seasons, unless they are being trained formally.

PRUNING TECHNIQUES

Always start with the removal of dead or damaged growth—often this is all the pruning that trees and shrubs will need. Depending on the plant, and the desired outcome, there are a few basic techniques which can be used for pruning.

Pinching involves removing the growing tip of a stem, forcing side shoots to be produced, and results in a compact, bushy plant. Pinching should not be performed when plants are about to flower.

Shearing is pinching on a large scale, using shears or scissors to shape the canopy, as in hedging and topiary. Not all plants can be effectively sheared—it works best on those with small leaves.

Cutting back, or heading back, shortens the branch to a desirable growing point without removing it entirely. This reduces the size of the plant, but also encourages it to grow more densely from the base.

Thinning involves the removal of whole stems or branches, cutting them at their origin or at ground level, as with some shrubs. Thinning removes old unproductive stems, and enhances the plant's structure, without reducing its overall size.

ESPALIERS

The technique of growing trees and shrubs as espaliers involves training the plants so that they grow with a flat branch structure, such as against walls or along wires. Espaliered shapes include fans, cordons, informal and palmette, and they especially suit fruit trees and shrubs like apples, pears and redcurrants. The technique encourages good crops, but is also decorative and doesn't require a lot of space.

STANDARDS

Trees and shrubs are also commonly trained as standards. A standard specimen has a single bare trunk with a rounded crown of foliage. Traditionally, the top growth was clipped into a ball—topiary style—but standards can also be more informal. Some trees can be grafted into standards with weeping canopies, so that the foliage grows from the top of the trunk and cascades down.

GLOSSARY

ACID SOIL: soil that has a pH of less than 7.

ALKALINE SOIL: soil that has a pH of greater than 7.

AXIL: the part of the plant where the leaf joins the stem.

BRACT: a modified leaf directly behind a flower or cluster of flowers; sometimes brightly coloured.

CALYX/CALYCES: the outer part of a flower; consisting of sepals and may be brightly coloured or decorative.

COMPOUND LEAF: a leaf made up of two or more leaflets.

COROLLA: the part of a flower that is formed by the petals.

CROWN: the top of the tree formed by the canopy; also the part of the plant where new shoots arise.

CULTIVAR: a distinct form of a plant with different features from the species; usually a result of selected breeding programs or cultivation.

CUTTING: a section of leaf, stem or root that is separated from a plant in order to reproduce it.

DEADHEADING: the removal of finished flowers in order to prevent seeds from forming, and to encourage the production of new blooms.

DECIDUOUS: a tree or shrub that loses its leaves annually and becomes dormant as part of its natural lifecycle.

DOUBLE FLOWER: a flower that has more petals than the usual number in the species.

EVERGREEN: a plant that retains its leaves throughout the year.

FAMILY: a group of related plants, including genera and species.

FLORET: a single flower in a composite arrangement or head of many flowers.

FROND: the large compound leaf of a fern, palm or cycad.

GENUS: closely related plants, within a family, that share many characteristics; includes species.

HABIT: the plant's usual form, appearance and way of growing.

HYBRID: a plant which is the result of crossing different genera, species or cultivars.

INFLORESCENCE: a flowering stem with more than one flower.

NODE: the part of a stem from which the leaf or bud grows.

PALMATE: a compound leaf with leaflets from a single point.

PANICLE: a branched raceme.

PEDICEL: the stalk of an individual flower.

PERENNIAL: a plant that lives for more than two years; in gardens, the term mostly applies to non-woody plants, but can also describe the habits of shrubs and trees.

RACEME: an unbranched flowering stem of stalked flowers, with the youngest at the top.

SEMI-EVERGREEN: a tree or shrub with habits that are between evergreen and deciduous; also called semi-deciduous.

SEPAL: a petal-like structure that forms part of the calyx.

SPECIES: very closely related plants, within a genus; the basic unit of classification.

TERMINAL: located at the end of a shoot or stem.

VARIEGATED: irregular colouring; a leaf that is naturally green but displays other colours.

VARIETY: a particular type of a plant that has different features from the species and occurs naturally.

WHORL: a circular arrangement of three or more leaves or flowers arising from a single point on the stem.

PHOTO
CREDITS

DELL ADAM: 38 top, 93.

BAY PICTURE LIBRARY: 67 bottom, 82, 154, 174, 197 top, 240, 294, 302, 303 bottom, 305 top, 318, 334 top R, 360 top, 361, 395, 426.

JOE FILSHIE: back cover (top and bottom L), 2, 30–1, 34, 35, 52, 74, 78 top, 94 bottom, 96–7, 98, 104, 106, 109, 110 (top R, bottom L and R), 114, 184–5, 189, 202, 205, 208 bottom, 210, 211 top L, 213, 218 top L, 230–1, 233, 235, 237 bottom, 238, 245 top, 248, 252, 253 top, 259, 260 (top L, bottom L and R), 264, 267, 380, 474 top L.

DENISE GREIG: 51, 99, 449, 452, 474 top R, 478 top L.

ANDRÉ MARTIN: front cover, 344–5, 490, 493.

MURDOCH BOOKS PHOTO LIBRARY: 43, 60, 128, 130–1, 134–5, 147, 148, 152, 153 top R, 164, 177, 178–9, 220–1, 232 top, 260 top R, 291, 325, 327 bottom, 360 bottom, 402 top, 410–11, 428 bottom, 437, 447, 454, 468–9.

LORNA ROSE: 6–7, 8, 11, 12, 16, 19, 20, 22–3, 26, 32–3, 36–7, 38 bottom, 39, 42, 48, 49 top, 53 bottom, 54–5, 56–7, 58–9, 61, 62–3, 64–5, 70–1, 72–3, 75 top R, 76–7, 78 bottom, 83, 84–5, 86–7, 89, 90–1, 94 top, 95, 100 bottom, 101, 103, 117, 118–19, 120–1, 122, 123, 124–5, 126–7, 129, 132, 136–7, 138, 139 top, 140–1, 142–3, 144–5, 146, 150–1, 153 top L, 155, 156–7, 158–9, 160–1, 162–3, 165, 166–7, 169, 171, 172 bottom, 173, 175, 176, 180–1, 183, 186–7, 188, 190–1, 192–3, 194–5, 196, 197 bottom, 199 bottom, 200–1, 203, 204,

206–7, 208 top, 209, 211 top R, 212, 214–15, 217, 218 bottom, 219, 222, 224–5, 226, 228–9, 236, 237 top, 239, 241, 242–3, 244, 245 bottom, 249, 250–1, 253 bottom, 254–5, 256–7, 268–9, 270–1, 272, 273, 274–5, 276–7, 278–9, 280–1, 282, 284–5, 286–7, 288–9, 290, 292–3, 295, 296, 297 top, 298–9, 300–1, 303 top, 304, 305 bottom, 306–7, 308–9, 310–11, 312–13, 314–15, 316–17, 319, 320–1, 322, 324, 327 top, 328–9, 330–1, 333, 334 (top L, bottom L and R), 336–7, 338, 341, 346, 347, 350–1, 352–3, 354–5, 356–7, 359, 362–3, 364–5, 366–7, 368–9, 370–1, 374–5, 376–7, 378–9, 382–3, 384–5, 386–7, 388–9, 390–1, 392, 394, 396–7, 398–9, 401, 402 bottom, 403, 404, 406–7, 408 bottom, 409, 412–13, 414, 415, 416–17, 418–19, 420–1, 422–3, 424–5, 427, 428 top, 429, 431, 432, 434, 436, 438, 440–1, 442–3, 444–5, 446, 448, 450–1, 453, 455, 456–7, 458–9, 460–1, 462–3, 464, 466–7, 471, 474 (bottom L and R), 476–7, 478 (top R, bottom L and R), 481.

SUE STUBBS: back cover (top R), 4, 25, 29, 49 bottom, 75 top L, 133, 172 top, 342–3, 435, 465, 482–3, 484, 487, 494.

PAT TAYLOR: 44.

JAMES YOUNG: 470.

THE PUBLISHER WOULD LIKE TO ACKNOWLEDGE PHOTOGRAPHY IN THE FOLLOWING GARDENS: Bebeah, Australia; Brackenback, New Zealand; Buskers End, Australia; Cherry Cottage, Australia; Craigie Lea, Australia; Dunedin, Australia; Eagleroo, Australia; Foxglove Spires, Australia; Greenlaw, Australia; Heronswood, Australia; Hillview, Australia; Kennerton Green, Australia; Kiah Park, Australia; Lambrigg, Australia; Lindfield Park, Australia; Merrygarth, Australia; Micalago Station, Australia; Moidart, Australia; Nooroo, Australia; Plassy, Australia; Titoki Point, New Zealand; Wombat Hill, Australia; Yengo, Australia.

INDEX

Murdoch Books® Australia
GPO Box 1203
Sydney NSW 2001
Phone: + 61 (0) 2 4352 7000
Fax: + 61 (0) 2 4352 7026

Murdoch Books UK Limited
Ferry House, 51–57 Lacy Road
Putney, London SW15 1PR
Phone: + 44 (0) 20 8355 1480
Fax: + 44 (0) 20 83551499

Published in 2003 by Murdoch Books®, a division of Murdoch Magazines Pty Ltd.
©Text, design, and photographs copyright Murdoch Books® 2003

Printed by Midas Printing (Asia) Ltd
PRINTED IN CHINA

National Library of Australia Cataloguing-in-Publication Data
Leong, Susin. Form & foliage guide to trees & shrubs.
Includes index. ISBN 1 74045 217 8. 1. Shrubs–Identification.
2. Trees–Identification. 3. Shrubs–Pictorial works.
4. Trees–Pictorial works. I. Loughlin, Tracy. II. Title. 582.16

Text: Susin Leong
Design: Tracy Loughlin
Design Concept: Marylouise Brammer
Creative Director: Marylouise Brammer
Editorial Director: Diana Hill
Production: Janis Barbi

Chief Executive: Juliet Rogers
Publisher: Kay Scarlett